What Others are S

Your True

YOUR TRUE VOICE *offers a unique approach to developing "free speech" and aligning with impeccability revealing the outrageous joy awaiting your heartfelt connection to life. The poetic wisdom and practices, thought provoking and fun, make a powerful awareness-building combo! Dielle encourages her reader towards loving responsibility for all aspects of our expression and helps us remember that when coming from the heart, whether you move quietly and speak in a whisper or sing out at the top of your lungs, your truth will echo through the cosmos with a roar!*
Gini Gentry, *Dreaming Heaven* co-creator, DVD and Journeybook

Dielle Ciesco masterfully invites us into the realm of resonance, vibration, toning and many other components of sound and voice. With expert guidance, we are encouraged to claim our authentic voice, to heal and breathe, and to enjoy the sounds of creation. YOUR TRUE VOICE *is engaging, accessible, and full of heart--a guide for vocal, emotional and spiritual healing. This workbook is packed with innovative methods that the author has personally used for years, tried and true techniques we can all learn to do. Ciesco's work also connects with spiritual and shamanic wisdom which adds layers of depth and meaning.*
Eric Myers, M.A., author of *The Astrology of Awakening Series*

Enter the gates of your authentic self through YOUR TRUE VOICE, *Dielle Ciesco's companion to her first book, The Unknown Mother, offers expert guidance to help both beginning explorers and advanced practitioners discover the untold wealth that dwells within the human*

voice. *Dielle's unique shamanic approach brings new insights to the field of natural voice work. Links to video instructions add to the usability of the many practices included in this valuable book.*
Susan Hale, author of *Sacred Space, Sacred Sound*

Dielle Ciesco has created an important resource for all readers, whatever their experience with their own voice thus far, to enter the world of transformational voice work. She touches on the essence of what the voice truly is in our world and gives us an easy to follow blueprint to discover the deeper layers to our own unique source of sound, creativity and healing. Informative, inspirational, and beautifully illustrated, YOUR TRUE VOICE *has the potential to change your life. A must have for anyone interested in understanding voice work as a life practice.*
Kara Johnstad, singer-songwriter, voice specialist and founder of Voice Your Essence™

The teachings in YOUR TRUE VOICE *offer an amazing journey for those interested in expressing themselves and engaging with the full power of the voice. The progression through the 10 Gates is well organized and adds a new level of integration and understanding of the concepts shared in Dielle's first book,* The Unknown Mother, *making this a great companion. The unique and powerful practices are a pleasure, sure to deepen the reader's experience with the whole voice for transformation that will last a lifetime.*
JoAnn Chambers (ShapeshifterDNA), cultural creative at Visionary Music and author of *The Sonic Keys: Sound, Light & Frequency*

YOUR TRUE VOICE

TOOLS TO EMBRACE A FULLY-EXPRESSED LIFE

YOUR TRUE VOICE

TOOLS TO EMBRACE A FULLY-EXPRESSED LIFE

DIELLE CIESCO

AYNI
BOOKS

Winchester, UK
Washington, USA

First published by Ayni Books, 2014
Ayni Books is an imprint of John Hunt Publishing Ltd., Laurel House, Station Approach,
Alresford, Hants, SO24 9JH, UK
office1@jhpbooks.net
www.johnhuntpublishing.com
www.ayni-books.com

For distributor details and how to order please visit the 'Ordering' section on our website.

Text copyright: Dielle Ciesco 2013

ISBN: 978 1 78279 558 2

A CIP catalogue record for this book is available from the British Library.

Design and illustrations: Stuart Davies
www.stuartdaviesart.com

Printed in the USA by Edwards Brothers Malloy

We operate a distinctive and ethical publishing philosophy in all
areas of our business, from our global network of authors to
production and worldwide distribution.

CONTENTS

This book is dedicated to Stuart, my Honey.

ACKNOWLEDGMENTS

I would like to take a moment to thank the kind and hard-working team at John Hunt Publishing for their support with this book, from editing to design to marketing.

I would also like to thank the people that have encouraged and inspired me to continue writing, especially those who having read my first book, desired a non-fiction companion for their own walk with Matrina. This is for you!

Most especially, I want to thank my husband, Stuart: You never fail to make me feel like your priority. I am truly blessed by you in countless ways.

I Give You My Word – A Message from the Goddess of Sound

What does it mean when we say, "I give you my word?" It is a promise, a vow that we are telling the truth, that we mean to follow through and will not disappoint. Look closely. We use the word "give" which refers to a gift, something shared. And we say, "my word" not "words". Why? Because we aren't talking about words as objects or units of meaning. We are talking about *the* word as power. We could say, "I give you the power of my words... I give you my faith."

Consider what typically happens when you read a self-help book. Do you usually finish reading the entire book or just peruse parts? Do you get very excited about the processes or ideas shared, motivated to apply them, but then move onto another book or project? Do you really put into practice the suggested exercises? No judgment necessary. Just consider your habits going in... because this book is different.

This book is alive. It senses your presence. It is meant to be like an apprenticeship with a wise teacher... the teacher being you. There is power on every page should you choose to open to receive it. In fact, this book is reading you just as you are reading it. It's in partnership with Life, and the three of you, whether you realize it or not, are colluding to give you exactly what you need. It will arrive, whether or not you follow through on the exercises. Your intent is enough to bring it to you. Will you be aware when it arrives or will the moment pass unrecognized?

This book assumes you've done enough work on yourself that you are far beyond blame and denial and really want to know the Truth. You now take responsibility for your own healing. You recognize that you are your own healer and that only the Truth will set you free. It isn't up to someone else to change so that you can be happy or to give you what you think you need. You are willing. YOU ARE THE MASTER!

This book is based on the 10 Gates of Sound as presented in the book, *The Unknown Mother: A Magical Walk with the Goddess of Sound*. In it, I mentor the character Wrenne as she walks the path to discover her True Voice. If you haven't read the book, that's quite okay. You can still begin your explorations with this material. But of course, I highly recommend you read the book at some point in order to fully integrate the wisdom it contains.

Throughout this book, each of the 10 Gates of Sound is presented with an attunement which is really the only thing you need to get started. Life will follow through on your behalf and present the rest of the lessons to you at the right moment and time. So even if you only ever skimmed each chapter but never actually practiced the specific practices listed, you are still bound to have the exact experiences you need to acquaint you with and move you through each gate. And hopefully, the little nudge you get from Life will be enough to bring you back here, to the relevant passages and practices.

That said, I hope you do read each chapter, savoring each letter, each word. After all, each of these practices has intrinsic value and can greatly ease any struggles that may arise. The gates offer a holographic landscape and holistic approach to coming into wellness. I hope you engage with each one and take time to journal about your experiences. I hope you work with enthusiasm and dedication, taking this as deeply as you can, submerging into bottomless oceans and emerging into new territory, all the while remembering that there is no one right way.

How does one demonstrate mastery? Through the practice of the art! Therefore, I present here many different practices that you can return to again and again on your journey. They aren't meant to be done only once or twice. They are meant to become a part of your bag of tricks, tools you reach for to access your Truth. Each time you return to a practice, you have the opportunity to discover something deeper, something new. If you can practice with a partner or in a group, all the better. By working with others on the same path, you deepen your ability to observe what remains subtle, broaden your own insights, and come to know yourself even better. Just don't forget that this is between you and you. It is neither a competition nor a contest.

In fact, each practitioner must find his or her own way to do each of the exercises provided in order to reap the most benefit. This work is meant to help you listen to, respect, and trust your Self.

Whether venturing solo or with others, this is your journey, your walk. Give yourself your word that you will give it your commitment, discipline your will, and always do your best. Open to the magic of Sound and receive all that Life has waiting in store for you.

Blessings,

Matrina

GOING FORWARD

You will need to acquire a notebook in which you can keep your observations, thoughts, experiences, and insights in working with this text. I suggest you find something special and just for this purpose. There are many decorative journals on the market, but you can always buy a simple spiral-bound notebook and decorate the cover yourself. There are also online journals, such as Penmia and Diary.com, available at no and low cost; think of the trees you'll be saving! I really like Penzu. It has a great free service and low-fee service with some really nice features including the ability to customize your journal and post via e-mail.

Once you've obtained your journal, begin by taking a moment to write about your hopes and dreams for this journey. Give yourself your word.

THE 1ST GATE

ATTUNEMENT

Adventure down the vocal tube through which all sounds we make arise
just like Alice as she tumbles, you too can change your size
Shrinking smaller into each atom, the ticket for admission
to witness the birth of sounds and words, springing from deep within
Find the marks of past traumas stored, energies distorted
residues of long forgotten expressions once aborted
Give these hungry ghosts their say and watch the river rise
removing implants, cleansing fears, bringing light to all the lies
This creative center awakens, giving voice to our feelings, ideas, and
*   dreams;*
now you are ready, initiation, to rip your cage's seams
So open up, let it out, sing out, "This sound is me!"
and celebrate the reclaiming of your voice with a capital V

THE VOCAL CHANNEL

For a very long time, the Voice has been patiently waiting for you to bring it into full consciousness. This is a call to awaken the lion that sleeps. You've been wielding your words like feathers for so long, when all along they were more like swords, piercing your mind with their poisoned tips, striking out at yourself and those you love and those who are different from you. For so long, you've accepted your universe and all of the concepts in it without question, unknowingly using words to fortify your dark and lonely castle when you could have used them to create a beautiful, inviting garden. For so long now, something else has held the power of the word and used it against you and the people you love. No more.

~The Unknown Mother

What exactly is the voice? If you had to define it, what would you say? That it is a person's ability to speak? That the voice is comprised of a larynx and vocal chords? That it is the unique sound that comes from a person, revealing his or her emotions, thoughts, and beliefs? In this book, the voice is all those things and more. It is multidimensional – physical, mental, emotional, and spiritual. It is a magical tool that we have come to take for granted. Let's rectify that by diving right in. In *The Unknown Mother*, Wrenne's journey starts with the vocal channel.

The vocal channel is an etheric tube (with certain physical manifestations such as the vocal chords) that begins (actually it doesn't "begin" anywhere, but we can say that it begins) to form right in front of the face in the area of the nose and mouth. It is the area of our exchange with the outside world. This is where concepts of all kinds enter us, which we either spit out or swallow, and the place where our concepts are expressed into the world. It then continues through the mouth, past the tongue, one of the strongest muscles in the body. The tongue is like a sentry that protects the vulnerable tissues of our throat and vocal mechanism which I like to refer to as a reproductive organ. After all, our ability to sound is a way we all, men and women, give birth to ideas. The tongue is programmed by our thoughts, beliefs, and choices to allow things to pass both inwardly and out

The Vocal Channnel

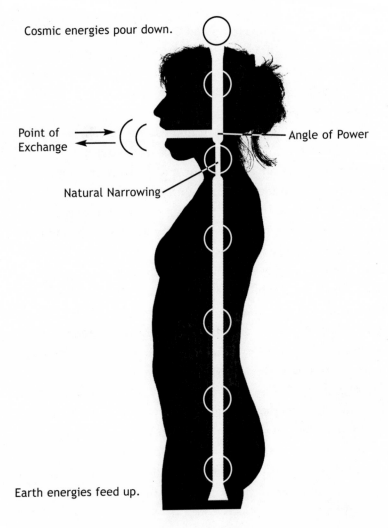

Cosmic energies pour down.

Point of Exchange

Angle of Power

Natural Narrowing

Earth energies feed up.

into the world… or not. Interestingly, its tissues grew from out of the heart during our development. We could theorize, then, that our tongue is a link to our heartfelt expressions, regardless of programming.

The channel hits the back of the throat at a 90-degree angle which is referred to as the *angle of power*. Just like a laser uses angles to shine a very precise beam that can cut, this angle in the throat can give the energy of our words a very piercing, clean momentum. At the *angle of power*, the channel splits, heading up into the head and out the crown and down into the body where it continues straight down, mirroring the esophagus, moving through the center of the lungs, the solar plexus, the belly, and deep into the dan tien or womb. Though the tube itself doesn't extend into the root chakra, its roots do receive and rely on energy from the root chakra and from the Earth herself, just as its branches take in the energy of the cosmos from above.

The vocal channel can both expand and contract, but typically, when we are quite young, we have our first experience with what I call "the clamp". We receive the very first message from our caretakers that we are not okay. Perhaps we are told to stop our bellyaching or to hush up. Maybe we get the message that we shouldn't be laughing in a serious environment or crying loudly in a jovial one. We might be told that what we've said has hurt someone else, and with that awareness, we begin to learn a new form of communication… one of lies, withholding, manipulation, and denial… a means of communication completely revered by our culture but not at all authentic to our nature.

This clamping message, reinforced throughout our lifetime by siblings, teachers, peers, friends, and the rest of society, begins to affect the flexibility of the vocal channel. We begin the lifelong habit of self-censure in order to be "appropriate" and "acceptable" and in order to control how others perceive us.

As we age and make poor choices that go against ourselves, the vocal tube freezes in place, and it narrows and congests like an artery. It becomes caked with choked-back cries, things we were afraid to say, ideas we've swallowed, and the beliefs that govern our expression, whether from this life or carried from previous ones. Our experiences with suppression, oppression, repression, and even depression – all the negative "pressions" – throughout our lives congeal within the energetic body creating disharmony and disease. One of the main goals of my Transformational Voicework (TV) is to cleanse the vocal channel of the IMpressions that have become part of our programming.

Just look at what is happening in our world right now. Whistleblowers like Assange and Snowden are villainized and persecuted for revealing, quite simply, the truth. In the meantime, liars and manipulators run our world governments, fattening their pockets and destroying our earth. There is little accountability. We were taught to prize image over substance, and the results are becoming clear. It is a smoky mirror pointing us inward to discover what I call True Voice – the voice that expresses as a clear channel of the Divine, the voice that tells it like it is without judgment, arrogance, or fear. It is the voice you were born to *be*.

I see more and more people desperate to recover their authenticity, creativity, and truth. These practices can help you develop your multidimensional voice into maturity. By connecting once again to True Voice, we can begin to trust ourselves and what wants to come out of us, more aware of distortions and adulterations, so we're less prone to manipulate... or be manipulated. And the way I see it, we must enter our adulthood as a species through selfhood, strength, inner wisdom and clarity or face our extinction.

From my own healing journey and in my experience working with hundreds of clients, it is clear that it simply isn't enough to mentally process our stuff. It isn't enough to say, "Okay, I'm going to change now." It may start there, but we also have to energetically process our habits, addictions, inherited traits, fears, pain and wounds through our nervous systems in order for lasting change to occur. We have to go *through* the fire… not just decide it isn't there still burning. Otherwise, the body remains the servant to old programming. And no, this isn't for the faint of heart. It is for the courageous and even desperate.

Working with the 10 Gates of Sound is the best way I know to make it through the fire. Sound is our mother, the creator of all that is, and in her boundless love for us, she provides opportunities for us to be nurtured at each of the gates. We begin by restoring the natural ability of the vocal channel to expand and contract at will, another thrust of TV. This is the way the vocal channel is meant to function. When the channel is narrowed consciously, it helps give a powerful, direct energy to our expression. We no longer need to rely on manipulative means of communication. Think back to the angle of power, and you get a sense of just how powerful and laser-like our words can be in this. What we express carries a power beyond the words we use!

When the channel is wide open, we are free to express whatever emotions we feel, no matter how large, when they take shape within us. We give them a wide girth, and we are done with them quickly as we return back to a neutral state of being. Think of the way in which an infant cries. The energetic stream of its emotions runs unimpeded through the vocal channel. It is thorough, and once expressed, complete. TV encourages a return to this kind of equanimity. Emotions come and go, whether positive or negative, so we don't attach to either. Nor do we blame others for these feelings. They are expressed cleanly and impersonally. We embrace all of our emotions without taking them personally.

As I've said, when the vocal channel is not under our conscious control, it can get stuck. When locked in a wide position, we are prone to histrionics or endless chitchat. Our emotions and need to stimulate rule us. When the vocal channel is stuck in a narrowed configuration, we are rather rigid and our words lack compassion and softness. We hold too much in and back, becoming very inhibited. You may see these aspects demonstrated in yourself or others.

Notice how the Vocal Channel mirrors the chakra system, the Tree of Life, and many other metaphysical structures. This is no coincidence. Nature knows what it is doing. We just have many interpretations of that nature because we are storytellers perceiving life from different points of view.

Your first task is to establish an awareness of this channel and all of the programming that clogs it. You will do this through journaling, visualizing, meditating, and paying attention to the things that synchronistically appear in your life (movies, conversations, situations) that carry a message related to this task as you work through the practices. Later, I will introduce my Transformational Voicework processes that help fully clear and then return normal functioning of the channel.

It is always important to drink plenty of water but especially so before and after these practices! Water helps us to flow with ease. It helps us to move fluidly past and beyond obstacles. It helps us let go. It carries away the wreckage of our emotional traumas.

In fact, call in all the elements as you work through these 10 Gates of Sound. I've already mentioned fire. Fire assists in our transformation, burning away the old. Air sweeps in and purifies; it refreshes and invigorates. Earth grounds and centers us, rooting us in our authenticity. And Ether provides the space in which everything occurs. It helps us stretch and grow into new territory.

You need do nothing extravagant or complicated. It is enough to close your eyes and think of each element. Just see a picture in your mind's eye. If this is difficult for you, find some outward symbol of each element... a candle, a cup of water, a feather, a stone... and encircle them with yarn or string. Of course, if you prefer to create an elaborate altar or do some other practice with the elements, that's fine too.

Take a few moments to consider how best to utilize the elements while working with this book. Record your thoughts in your journal.

MIRROR WORK

When working with my "not-just-Toltec" Toltec teacher and mentor, I engaged in practices in which we worked with mirrors. We'd sit in front of our own mirrors and gaze, playing with reality and shifting our perceptions. I found it to be quite powerful, so I'm not surprised this practice has found its way into Transformational Voicework. In *The Unknown Mother*, Wrenne first encounters Matrina when meditating in front of her mirror. Mirror work has now become an ever-evolving and powerful tool in TV.

For many people, staring at themselves in a mirror is a very difficult practice. We are afraid to look into our own eyes for what we might find there, what we might feel. Tendencies towards self-hatred or judgment can become magnified, and while this may seem at first to be counterproductive, it is actually quite clearing and absolutely necessary (*through the fire!*) in order to reach a state of complete self-acceptance with our visage. Once we work through our resistance, we gain access to all kinds of windows into our souls.

So, let's work with several mirror exercises. After each one, pause and give yourself some reflection time (no pun intended) with your journal.

PRACTICE ONE

Try your own mirror meditation. Provide yourself a distraction-free environment for at least twenty minutes and seat yourself in front of a large mirror. The closer you can be to it the better. You may want to do this at night with just a candle for light. As you sit before your own image, tune into your breathing and relax. Simply commune with yourself, looking deeply into your own eyes, or gazing gently into and through the "big picture". Notice your reactions. How does it feel? Are you comfortable? Feeling awkward? Stuck on some perceived imperfection? What are your eyes saying to you? What tracks of thought play in the background? Does your image morph and change? Do you feel love for the being before you?

PRACTICE TWO

Repeat your mirror meditation. Only this time, open your mouth and gaze down the Vocal Channel. Breathe through your mouth. Notice your jaw. Is it tight? See if you can bring relaxation to it. Simply drop the jaw, as if there was a weight pulling it down without effort. Look inside your mouth. Notice your tongue and its strength. It is, in fact, one of the strongest muscles in the body. Is it rising up, lying flat, tense or obscuring your view? Can you relax your tongue, dropping it down as if starting a yawn and open the back of your throat? How does it feel? As you continue to gaze, notice the color, temperature, sensitivity, and texture of the tissues that line the back of your throat. Notice everything about it. How does it feel to be giving this area your full attention? Are you tense? Can you relax? Close your jaw if it feels stressed and give it a rest. Then go back in again. Yawn if you feel like it. Then go back in. Feel deeply. Remember, in both men and women, our vocal mechanism is a reproductive organ. We give birth to our words, our truth, here. If you feel vulnerable, you are not alone. You are giving this hidden, tender center exposure. Send it the information that it is safe, loved, appreciated, respected, supported, and healed. Give it your permission to come to new life.

PRACTICE THREE

Now that you are comfortable with gazing into your mouth, let us move even deeper into the Vocal Channel, using your imagination, your capacity to dream, to see deep into the vocal mechanism. You may do this with your eyes open or closed, but leave your mouth open if you can. If your eyes are open, remain sitting. If you close your eyes, you may lie down, but only if you know you won't fall asleep. As you begin to travel with your awareness down the Vocal Channel, notice any irritations, discolorations, splotches, kinks, or distortions of energy. Allow these things to be revealed. Intend to discover the stories of humanity's past that resonate with your throat center. (Whether or not you believe in past lives literally, consider your ancestry, periods of time that interest you, histories that fascinate or scare you.) Simply let things arise in your mind's eye. "Remember" incidents that you carry with you today that affect your ability to communicate or speak your truth. Notice patterns. Be open to new insights and messages from your higher self. Pay special attention to throat-related traumas such as hangings, tongue cuttings, and head-choppings. Notice if any of your cells respond to these thoughts either subtly or palpably. No need to fear. You are not reliving such traumas. You are simply bringing the light of your awareness to them. You are seeing how such traumas have impacted our human potential. You are deciding, "No more!" If a memory or feeling resonates deeply, follow it. Give it voice if necessary. Use your imagination to see it, release it, or dress it and heal it.

PRACTICE FOUR

Prepare yourself for another journey through the vocal channel. This time as we travel, bring your awareness to all of the holdings of this lifetime. Remember times you held back, felt guilty or ashamed because of something you said, or times you were afraid to speak up for yourself or others. Bring to mind all the hurts swallowed, all the injustices ignored, all the pain or even laughter squelched. Feel the long dead energies of these remnants stirring and yawning awake. Let that lump in your throat rise up to the surface. Feel the screams, the cries, the songs, laughter, the curses, the proclamations of love rising and releasing into the light. If a memory or feeling resonates deeply, follow it. Give it voice if necessary. Expel old programming and restore your pure self to yourself. Let go of what has been holding you back, fanning the flames of your fears or misguided beliefs about yourself, your voice, and the power of your creative expression. Make a new promise to yourself. Create a new belief... one that encourages and honors your Truth.

Remember, nothing here has the power to hurt you. It may be uncomfortable for a time or bring up painful feelings, but given your time and tenderness, they will move up and out. There are many ways to support yourself in dealing actively and effectively with anything that may arise. Remember to invoke the elements. Yoga, bodywork, cleansing diets, salt or clay baths, herbs, flower essences, essential oils, meditation and energy work can all assist your body and mind with the healing process. There are many levels of this work. If you are serious about going all the way, you may find it very difficult to do alone. You may want to work directly with someone or in a group setting with like-minded spiritual warriors.

... she struck me lightly but briskly on the back. With theasurprise, time and space collapsed. The room disappeared around me, and nothing remained to help me orient myself. I was thrust down a tunnel, spinning and flailing. I emerged as a woman in an old German village, wearing a torturous device on my head that painfully pulled my tongue out of my mouth and made it impossible for me to speak. I saw myself as a spy, and they were cutting my tongue right out of my mouth. I then saw life after life of gruesome torture and punishment for speaking, praying, expressing, preaching, and practicing various arts that had been deemed heretical, evil, dangerous, or just oppositional. And it didn't stop with tongue trauma. I saw others experience throat

cuttings, hangings, burnings, dunkings, and beheadings. Over many lifetimes, I was both the persecuted and the persecutor.

~The Unknown Mother

PRACTICE FIVE

In *The Unknown Mother*, Matrina offers Wrenne a life-changing activation of her throat center. It is time to activate yours. This ritual is not to be taken lightly. Plan a special day for it well in advance. Decide where you want to be... inside, outside in nature, at home, in a power spot. How will you create sacred space for yourself? With candles? With incense? With flowers? Decide if you want to be alone or have a witness. Decide what you will intentionally do both before the activation to prepare for it, such as anoint yourself with oils or drink a special tea, and after the activation to integrate it, such as take a bath or a sunny nap. Read over the activation below and have a sense of the flow so that you can perform it smoothly referring to the text as necessary.

ACTIVATION

Inhale one deep breath and release it deliberately and evenly. Prepare to give to yourself. Now gently tip your chin towards the ceiling as far up as is comfortable for you. Holding your head in this upward tilted position, keep your neck long and stretched.

Now inhale and hold your breath at the top. With your breath held, see if you can tense and release your stomach muscles, pumping your stomach in and out with the breath held. Continue. Now exhale, and with the breath held out begin to pump your stomach in and out.

Now gently bring your head back, bringing your chin down to rest on your chest, stretching the back of the neck. In this position, breathe in and begin to pump your stomach. Exhale. Pump your stomach with the breath held out. Good. Gently bring your head back to center and turn your head slowly right looking behind you and then slowly left. Good.

Prepare to receive. Now with your head center again, relax and release any tension you are holding. Bring your attention to the area of the throat where that little "v" is at the base of your neck. This precious energy pool is known as the center for decisions to the Toltec wisdom-keepers. Within that chalice, see a liquid light glowing and radiating, upward and outward like a pulsar. As you focus on this light, it becomes warm and golden as it begins to drip like honey, up, down and in all directions coating and soaking into every tissue, bone, cell... of your throat, neck, larynx, vocal folds, tongue, thyroid, parathyroid... everything relaxes.

The deepest of holdings, most rooted obstructions, secret longings and most insistent fears are being penetrated by this light. Muscles twitch with the release of past trauma, betrayal, heartache, and despair. It is transmuted effortlessly in this golden light. Energy is moving now, pulsing... it is free and alive. The wheel at your throat is spinning and opening like a colorful pinwheel riding the breeze, a kaleidoscope of colors, every color of the spectrum, there in your very own voice.

Now imagine the entire channel of your throat suddenly reveals itself as a crystal palace, the very walls of your throat clear and transparent, radiating light. And as each color of the rainbow is refracted by the prism of your vocal mechanism, a glorious, victorious white light breaks through emanating outward. Your entire body smiles with joy and relief! From this place, staying very deep, very connected, repeat each letter of the alphabet: A, B, C... reprogramming each letter that forms all your thoughts, words, ideas, and dreams.

THE 2ND GATE

ATTUNEMENT

In and out, we breathe without trying... all through life, until we are dying. Taking Life in, then letting it go... an indelible mystery unfolds as we grow. Beyond the mere physical process of breathing... something breathes us as if it were weaving. With each inhalation, we are filled with True Light... and with each exhalation, we again have clear sight. In and out, like the tides of the ocean... reborn by our own breath's magical potion. We don't even know the depth of this exchange... inhaling the same molecules of our ancestors again and again. In and out, we both give and receive... in an endless exchange, we continue to weave. Life moves in and life moves out... as we move through this dreamscape, dancing about. If we are aware of how we are breathing, we become choosers of all we are dreaming.

BREATHWORK

Not many of us remember our first gulp of air. How wonderful it must have been, to finally breathe on our own. Our first act of power in our new world. We establish patterns of breathing at an early age. If we were often fearful or timid, then our breathing is more likely to be shallow. If we were athletic or played a wind instrument, then perhaps we developed a more robust lung capacity. But if we also took on the habit of smoking, chances are we lost that capacity. If we struggled with allergies or grew up in a home full of cigarette smoke, we might have trained ourselves to take in no more air than was absolutely necessary to sustain life. We may have missed out on a higher level of oxygenation, never even knowing what we were missing.

I first became aware of the power of the breath at a Noetics conference in Orlando, Florida where I lived at the time. A lovely woman in one of the workshops gifted me with a song she'd written. I don't know what happened to that woman, but I do still have the scrap of paper on which she wrote the lyrics about breathing in and out to find your soul. It was a beautiful message that I must have needed to hear.

This message was later confirmed through a transformational practice known as recapitulation which is now incorporated into my Transformational Voicework. Recapitulation is the process of using the breath to reclaim lost energy held in certain memories or experiences from our past. Many students of shamanism will spend years of their lives on this one practice... some even making it their life's work. I myself made it a regular part of my day for many of the years I was studying Toltec Shamanism and return to it as needed to this day.

I've had some pretty incredible experiences with recapitulation. I can remember getting up from a session and feeling as though I was in a completely different body. It took me some time to remember how to function. I've also had the experiences of both feeling 20 pounds heavier and 20 pounds lighter after practicing. Clients have reported similar experiences after TV sessions.

A WORD ABOUT RECAPITULATION

I have not included traditional Recapitulation as a practice in this book because it really lies outside the scope of this work. If you would like to know more about it, I suggest you look into the many good books on the topic including:

Mastery of Awareness: Living the Agreements by doña Bernadette Vigil

Toltec Recapitulation: Reclaiming the Beauty and Mystery of the Present Moment by Raven Smith

The Toltec Path of Recapitulation: Healing Your Past to Free Your Soul by Victor Sanchez

The Toltec Way: A Guide to Personal Transformation by Dr. Susan Gregg

---

This gate is all about the breath. The practices will help you become aware of your breathing and gain insights into your habits. Who knows? You may have some amazing experiences too. Reaffirm your commitment to yourself and your journey as you begin.

Bear in mind that breathwork can be taxing, especially after a lifetime of bad habits. Please take it easy and honor your body and its needs. You may do these exercises sitting or standing.

A word of caution: Breathwork can be incredibly invigorating but extremely taxing if you aren't used to it. Please be wise. Everyone's capacities are different. Honor your body and what it is telling you in every moment. If you have any health conditions that affect your breathing, please consult with your physician before trying the more vigorous of these and any subsequent exercises.

Practice One

Breaking Out

As you breathe in, imagine you are rolled very tightly as if in a corset. This device, however, compresses you from as high as your shoulders to down below your waist. Maybe we should call it a straightjacket. Feel the tension, the weight, the discomfort as you breathe. Notice the extent of the constriction and its impact upon your breathing. Now, in one swift inhalation, use your breath to begin to loosen this "corset". Feel your breath pushing outward against the constriction, and as you do so, you create space to move. Use your focus to systematically feel the various areas, waist, shoulders, ribs, belly, chest, expanding more and more. Imagine and then feel the expansion all the way down to your toes. Allow the relief and "full-filled" breath to expand easily as the remnants of the corset finally drop away, tatters at your feet.

What have you come to realize as a result of doing this exercise? What are the effects of the images we are working with here? Are there situations in your life in which you don a corset and fail to breathe fully?

PRACTICE TWO

LONG DEEP BREATHING

Long, deep breathing is natural breathing... the way a baby breathes... the way you used to breath. Begin by emptying the lungs of air. When you inhale, fill your belly, then the area of the middle rib cage moving up into the chest. To exhale, pull the naval back towards the spine in the belly area, contracting and expelling air in the chest, rib region and then belly. Practice this for a while taking note of how you feel. Then try a variation by releasing first the belly, then the ribs, and finally the chest. Do this for several cycles comparing the two. Then try releasing everything at once in one measured exhalation.

How did that feel? Which of these techniques felt the most comfortable? What else have you noticed?

PRACTICE THREE

FOLLOW YOUR BREATH

This next exercise will be done in three parts. First sitting and breathing, just watch your breath. Don't try to change anything. Just notice the beginning and ending of each cycle of the breath. Can you tell where one begins and one ends?

After a while, practice shifting the attention of your breathing while doing the long, deep breathing pattern of Practice Two, breathing in from the belly upward and exhaling from the chest down. Breathe in and focus on the inhalation even as you then exhale. Put all your attention on the inhalation and just await the next breath in. Notice how the inhalation becomes deeper and longer?

Now reverse. Place your focus on the exhalation. When you inhale, be awaiting the next exhalation. Exhale. Exhale. Notice how your exhalation deepens and lengthens?

Write in your journal any observations or realizations you've had since starting these breathing practices.

PRACTICE FOUR

ENHANCED EXHALATION

Commence deep breathing. At the bottom of each exhalation, you are going to squeeze every last bit of air from your lungs like you are squeezing the air out of an air mattress to store it back in its original packaging. Squeeze. Squeeze. Hold the breath out, hold it, hold it, and then inhale. Ah! Relief! Experiment with the length of the holding, but remember, this isn't an endurance test. Always honor your body's capabilities and go gently.

Have you been able to keep things gentle and easy? Have you noticed any challenges to breathing? What does it feel like to hold the breath? What emotions, if any, arise?

PRACTICE FIVE

LET LIFE BREATHE YOU

Really, we think we are the ones breathing, but breathing is a mysterious force. The only thing we ever do is restrict, constrict, or resist this force. So in this next exercise, do nothing. Don't breathe! Let the breath happen. Feel the breath filling you up and then withdrawing. When you are comfortable with the idea of effortless breathing, imagine that each breath is actually love. Feel that love penetrating you, enlivening each cell, enriching your blood, flowing all around and within you.

What does it feel like to breathe in this way? Can you imagine employing this breath during a stressful situation? What do you think would happen? How would it impact you? Do you think it would impact others?

PRACTICE SIX

BREATH OF FIRE

The next exercise is a yoga breathing technique. First, imagine you are a dog in the hot sun and begin to pant. Once you've gotten the hang of that feeling, your belly moving in and out with each breath, close your mouth, and continue the same breathing pattern through the nose. You should still feel your diaphragm working... in, out, in, out. Going slowly is perfectly okay, but try speeding up when you are ready.

Remember, just do your best. If it is uncomfortable, you may be trying to do better than your best. Ease up.

Do you become easily winded when practicing this breath? Why do you think that is? Does this breath bring up any unusual sensations or feelings?

PRACTICE SEVEN

REBALANCING

The next Kundalini breathing exercise is for rebalancing. Place your fingers in the Hakini Mudra with each of the fingertips touching and the hands at sternum level. Your eyes focus gently downward, not all the way closed. Inhale in 8 short parts

through the nose and then exhale in 8 short parts through the mouth. The rhythm should be nice and relaxed. Continue and record your observations.

Are you finding it becoming easier to relax as you breathe? What impact did the mudra have on you as you practiced? Did you modify the exercise in any way? If so, why?

PRACTICE EIGHT

HumAzing!

Let's add some toning to your breathing and begin to warm up those vocal chords. First take note of how you are feeling in your body, mind and spirit. Breathe normally, and as you exhale, begin to make the "mmm" sound on the exhalation. Be free and easy. Allow yourself your own natural pace. Relax. After a couple of minutes, work through various combinations of vowels with that "mmm": MA MAE ME MO MOO. You can hold each of these one at a time for a single exhalation. MAAAAAA...

Add some variations and be as playful as you want: MOO-AH, MOO-AY, MOO-EE, MOO-OH, MOO-OH-AH, MOO-EE-AY.

Experiment with humming the entire vowel string on one exhalation.

How do you feel now? Are you having any thoughts about "doing it right"? How does it feel to engage the voice?

PRACTICE NINE

HumAzing Grace!

Let's now use the sound OM. OM is a Sanskrit syllable that points to all of existence, beyond time and space. It is a sound that realigns us with our divine nature.

When working with the tone of OM, one should give equal time to the O and the M. It doesn't have to be one long, sustained OM. In fact, I often prefer a pulsing series of short OMs from one exhalation. Experiment and see what works for you.

Begin by breathing in and out through the nose while only thinking the sound OM. After a few moments, begin to OM aloud on each exhalation. As mentioned, you can do a single OM for each exhalation or a series of pulses. As you breathe in, hear the sound of OM continue to pulse in your mind. Repeat this gentle toning for several minutes and then enjoy the benefits of the reverberation as you sit in stillness for several moments.

Journal anything that comes to you after practicing this breath. You might even want to draw a picture.

Remember, the breath is the current that links the human with the Divine. Can you see how its rhythm affects your mind and physical body? The breath can be your tool to break up congestion and stagnation. It also supports our sound; our ability to control our breath is directly related to the duration, power, and quality of our tones.

THE 3RD GATE

ATTUNEMENT

Alpha
Bet
consonants and vowels
a holographic universe
vibrating with sounds
with energies and manifestations
with vitalized breath
we enter into these mysteries
from birth unto death
channels and symbols
vessels and lights
combined and permutated
flying letter sprites
canoes in Life's stream
in rapids or stills
the units of a dream
can steal our will
so don't just accept
what's handed to you
design your own landscape
make your own true

THE ALPHABET

Every word in the English-speaking world, every single one, was made up using the same 26 letters!... War & Peace, *the Bible,* Little Women, *and even the latest issue of* Vogue *were all written with just 26 letters... Maybe [these pieces] were once part of a greater whole. Maybe working with them consciously helps us remember who and what we truly are: mysteries.*

~*The Unknown Mother*

A VERY BRIEF HISTORY OF THE ALPHABET

The alphabet can be described as a set of symbols that represents the sounds of speech in any particular language. There are really only speculations as to how the alphabet came to be. No one really knows the true story, though the Phoenicians are credited with having developed the very first alphabet. Whatever its roots, it is truly an amazing tool. Rather than write my own creation myth about the origins of the alphabet (hmm... sounds like fun), let me just say that over the centuries, the alphabet has been through countless revisions and alterations since its Phoenetic inception. I wonder when it stagnated to become the fixed alphabet we all know and love. Oh, and toning lovers of the world, we can thank the Greeks for introducing vowels into the mix.

In many of the mystery schools of various cultures, the letters of the alphabet are held as sacred vessels, used in meditations, and considered keys to the doorways of consciousness. In the modern age, most of us simply take the letters of the words we speak for granted, giving their potentials or inherent power virtually no consideration.

Have you ever taken a moment, since elementary school, to recite the alphabet? Have you ever felt the shape of the letters as they roll off your tongue? Have you ever noticed how we cannot name the consonants without also sounding a vowel? For example, we can only pronounce the letter "B" with the vowel "E". Even pronouncing the "B" sound without actually naming the letter requires us to attach an "UH" sound at the end. Have you noticed that certain letters are actually comprised of the combined sounds of other letters, a prime example being "Y"? Have you ever noticed how certain words starting with the same letter have a similar power... love and light for example?

In *The Unknown Mother: A Magical Walk with the Goddess of Sound*, letters are one of the 10 Gates of Sound. One of Wrenne's early lessons with her mystical guide revolves around the hidden significance of the letters of the alphabet. She meditates with these letters after realizing that every single book ever written is written with the same mere twenty-six letters of the alphabet. She discovers that each letter can be programmed with intent so that everything she speaks becomes a spell for harmony and wisdom.

This world is vibration. Vibration is the world. Everything, from the ant on the sidewalk to the thought in your head, is made of vibration. The letters of the alphabet, too, are little parcels of vibration, energies encapsulated in symbol. Sure, they carry certain residual and archetypal energies of our history, but they can also be programmed with love. We can work with them to receive their secrets.

Imagine if you decided what potent power the letter "A" might hold for you. Perhaps it will be a symbol of the element of air, bringing more movement into your life, clearing stagnation. Or perhaps it would represent appreciation bringing that quality to all with whom you spoke. Imagine if every word you spoke that contained the letter "A" from now on radiated with fresh *air* and *appreciation*! Now imagine taking each letter of the alphabet and programming it with your intent to generate the energies and qualities that would support you and others. Whether you spoke, prayed, sang or wrote, you would be transmitting these heavenly energies.

There are numerous ways to work with the letters of the alphabet in order to tap into their inherent qualities limited only by your creativity. You can obviously recite them, as we have all learned to do, or you can tone each letter instead. You can meditate with each letter using American Sign Language to get you in touch with a new dimension of each letter's power. You can write the letters out, meditating on the shape and feel of them. Recite a letter before bedtime; then watch for clues to the energy of that letter in your dreams. You can even dance the alphabet! Explore and discover for yourself the gifts these parcels contain.

What are your thoughts on this brief history? Have you ever considered that the letters of the alphabet may be more than they appear to be? What questions are you holding?

PRACTICE ONE

The following are suggestions for working with the alphabet meditatively. Try one or all of them and discover for yourself the hidden power within our letters. Please be in a comfortable meditative posture and a relaxed, receptive state when you practice.

- Recite each letter of the alphabet with your full attention.
- Recite and form the American Sign Language symbol for each letter of the alphabet. Pay attention to the shape of the letter, both in the fingers and when written as well as the sound of the letter, and how those two relate.
- Sing the alphabet song. Take your time and really feel each letter.
- Recite each vowel of the alphabet and each sound it makes.
- Recite each consonant of the alphabet followed by each vowel sound.

- Recite each letter of the alphabet and stream of consciousness-ly speak words beginning with each letter.
- Tone each letter of the alphabet accompanying each consonant with the vowel of your choice.
- Recite each letter of the alphabet while visualizing its written symbol.
- Recite each letter of the alphabet while writing its written symbol (in ink in sand, with paint, etc.).
- Focus on one letter for a week or longer. Search your environment for your chosen letter.
- Recite a particular letter before drifting off to sleep. Pay attention to your dreams.
- Notice what letter foods you eat start with. Apple. A. Recite the letter. Taste the apple.
- Place your palm over the written letter and feel the vibration of the letter. Compare letters.
- Choose to infuse letters with special meanings and qualities. For example, infuse the letter "C" with courage.
- Make a list of words you dislike or that trigger a negative response on paper. Put the list in a bowl and treat it with L-O-V-E. Love (or forgiveness or compassion, etc.).
- Consider the books on your bookshelf. Each written with the same 26 letters of the alphabet.
- Write the letters of the alphabet on the beach and allow the waves to wash them away.
- Silently form the America Sign Language sign for each letter of the alphabet. Try not to think. Just feel.
- Offer up a stone for each alphabet letter to a deity or teacher you revere.
- Tone/sound each letter from deep inside, feeling it first. Add one of the breathing techniques from the 2nd Gate.
- Write the alphabet forwards and backwards.
- Practice permutations of words. For example, how many different arrangements can be made from the letters of

PLAY (LAYP, AYPL, etc.).

- Feel for the four layers of speech. Matrina mentioned these in *The Unknown Mother*: "The Nada – yes, the All Sound. There are four dimensions of sound. The Vaikhari or coarse sounds we hear with our ears. Madhyama or mental sounds – the voices in our heads. Pashyanti or dream sounds. And then Para or transcendent sounds beyond the senses."
- Mix and match any combination of meditations.

Whichever of these exercises you have chosen to do, be sure to spend some time with your journal recording your experiences. Also consider writing about the practices you may not have chosen to do! Have you noticed any synchronicities in your life as a result of working with the letters in this way or with any of the other practices you've done within these pages?

PRACTICE TWO

I was unsure whether or not to include the results of my alphabet meditations, knowing all too well that what is true for me is not necessarily true for anyone else. I certainly don't want to influence or inhibit your own perceptions of the energies within the letters. At the same time, sharing them gives you a more complete illustration of the process I went through and may serve as inspiration to create your own list. So peruse the following with curiosity, not as the authoritative definitive... which nothing in *this* world is.

If we were eight years old, I might say to you, "I've invented a new game with the alphabet. Want to play?" Once we become adults, we forget that we are still just playing. We get very serious about the things we create, the methods and processes we develop. We want other people to take us seriously, to see us as authorities with very special offerings, and we fall into the trap of believing ourselves and the invented worlds we've created. So, I say to you now, "Want to play?"

A is the first letter of the Alphabet. A is equally rooted to heaven and earth. It is the letter of prayer. Utter A and you pray. A is pristine. Amen. Alleluia. Allah. Apu. Abracadabra. Awaken!

B is the second letter of the alphabet. B is the Big Bang. It is the instantaneous, spontaneous presence. B is birth. The Belly. Beloved. Being. Balance.

C is the third letter of the alphabet. I "C". C is Clarity, Clairvoyance, Creativity, Communion, and Communication.

D is the fourth letter and "of the light". It reminds us that even in Death and Destruction lies the Divine. In Discovery, Duality, Delicious, Destiny, Delight, DNA.

E Ejects the myth of our imperfection. It is Elation, Elevated, Evolution, Essence, Essentials, Ether. WEEE!!!

F is the 6th letter. Fluidity. eFFortless, Faith, Freedom, Fairies, Feminine, Flowers.

G is Genuine and Golden. Go, Great, God, Generosity, Gratitude, Giving, Glee.

H is the strength of Heave-Ho. It is High, Happiness, Hope, History, Hush.

I All seeing. All being. I is Independence, Isolation, Ignorance, Insight, Infinite, Immortality.

J is the 10th letter of the alphabet. Its energy is soft, but its strength is beyond measure. It is Jewel, Joy, Jai, Jolly.

K the 11th letter, is the Key to non-judgment and a loving attitude towards all. It is "oKay". It is a free flying Kite, a Kaleidoscope of colors, and a world full of butterfly Kisses.

L is the letter of Life that carries Love and Lessons. It is the call of Leadership and Legends.

M Lucky 13. Myth, Magic and Mystery. The hum of the

Mother, Mastery, Music.

N Negate the Negative and you have a positive. The power of No and the dream of Neverland. The Null and void is the comfy Nest in which we rest.

O is whole. All outside the O is represented equally with all that is inside the O. Opulence, Originality, Octave, Ocean.

Q is a fanciful letter, both elegant and challenging to the status Quo. Queen, Quest, Quiet, freQuency.

R is the 18th letter of the alphabet. It is Radiant, Royal, and overflowing with infoRmation from other dimensions.

S Slips and Slides and Saturates. Silence, Senses, Salvation, Soothe.

T A holy cross, a Tower of strength. Trust, Truth, inTent, Treasure.

U are the grail, the chalice that holds the ether. Underworld. Understanding. Unity. Uterus.

V is the 22nd letter of the alphabet and is the Voice of God. It is a Vessel in which Validation and Victory are poured.

W is the 23rd letter of the alphabet. W is a gentle sWooping line connecting point A to point B. W is the invisible connection between the millions of fragments that came from the One. We. Wonder. Willpower. Wellbeing. Whole. Water.

X is the 24th letter of the alphabet. X marks the spot, eXploration, eXperience, Xray.

Y our 25th letter is Yes. It is the arms stretched overhead accepting all the gifts of Heaven. Yay!

Z is the 26th and final letter of the alphabet. Z is the great leveler. It returns all back to A... the pristine and pure prayer, Zen. Zero.

Your journal is your place to begin your own alphabet meditation, turning each letter into an angel, or messenger that carries your light and intent. Be playful! Take your time. Enjoy the process and discovery.

PRACTICE THREE

WHAT IS A SIGIL?

Letters represent units of sound and so much more. There are consonants and vowels, each with their own unique energetic signature and ability to carry and transmit energy. Now you are beginning to see how working consciously with these units transforms the ordinary into the mystical. Sigil magic is yet another tool for working consciously with letters.

According to Austin Osman Spare, author of *The Book of Pleasure: The Psychology of Ecstasy*:

> *Sigils are monograms of thought... symbolizing desire and giving it form that has the virtue of preventing any thought on that particular desire, escaping the detection of the Ego, so that it does not restrain or attach such desire to its own transitory images, memories and worries, but allows it free passage to the sub-consciousness.*

Similar in nature to a spell or talisman, a sigil is a glyph infused with magical properties that we give it and also magical properties from assisting beings and realms when we ask for their support. In other words, we can ask for the support of our ancestors, angels, guides, or ascended masters when we create sigils.

Symbols are very dear to us. They convey a message without verbiage. Some symbols have a negative connotation, like the swastika, and others positive, like the cross. Of course, everyone is going to respond to a symbol based on what they've been taught about it and what they've experienced. The swastika is a perfect example. In Tibet, this symbol is considered one of great fortune. It is painted over doorways and elsewhere and evokes something positive.

Those of you with training in Reiki already understand the

power of such symbols in bringing about powerful energetic shifts. The Cho Ku Rei and Sei Hei Ki, for example, both used in the application of Reiki, are symbols imbued with great healing energies that can be invoked and used as needed. Sigils are just more personalized forms of such symbols and generally only used once.

Sigils are typically constructed using the letters of the alphabet which in and of themselves have tremendous energy and potential as I've already mentioned. When we combine these letters with imagination and intent, we are wielding our most powerful creative tools together.

Since it bypasses the conscious mind and all the things that get in the way of manifesting our desires, such as conflicting intentions, limited programming, fear-based thoughts, and the like, the sigil is able to influence the subconscious mind and hence bring about the desired result purely as a matter of faith. Our efforts go into creating the sigil, but then we detach and let universal forces answer our desire. In this way we give less energy to trying, overthinking, forcing, or debating our own self-sabotaging thoughts.

This occurs through the power of Intent which is in many ways comparable to the force of Faith. If you ever wonder where your faith lies, look around you. What do you see? The life you are living and the people in it reveal to you where you have chosen to store your faith. Reclaiming our faith from outdated patterns and habits takes years of very diligent practice... whatever the practice. It takes focus, determination, self-awareness, and open-mindedness to begin to create intentionally with the full force of our faith at our disposal. I'll talk about this a little more later on.

Sigils are really just representations of our intent, but they also serve as repositories of that intent. Think of them as little safe deposit boxes in which you keep your most precious thoughts and desires safe from negative thoughts and self-sabotage. Sigils are customized works of craftsmanship designed to bring about a specific intent. Here, I'll lead you through that process in five easy steps. Once you learn it, you can use it again and again to create sigils that meet your immediate needs.

Sigils are also a practice in non-attachment, as the sigil itself is usually (but not always) destroyed or forgotten. It is reminiscent of a sand painting, meticulously created only to be destroyed. It is the creative act and not the end result that receives our energy. In this way, a sigil is also a work of art, unique to its creator, originating from the power of one's imagination and word. It is an entire statement of intent compacted into a more potent, single form.

It is easy to create and requires only a clear, unbending intent. I say only, but again, developing unbending intent is something that takes much effort and practice. It requires taking responsibility for our thoughts and deeds, emotions and experiences. One way you can work on developing your intent includes simply setting goals and meeting them. They can be really small; just don't let yourself off the hook. If you say, "I'm going to meditate for 30 minutes today," then don't let your head hit the pillow until you've done it. Honor your commitments. Stay true to yourself.

For those of you interested in developing your intent, I suggest you investigate the shamanic practice of recapitulation mentioned at Gate 2. It is one of the most powerful ways I know to cleanse your energy and hone your intent. Dreamwork is another field of practice you might consider as is anything physically demanding such as Yoga or Tensegrity. Anything that requires discipline and focus can help you develop your intent.

How do I make a Sigil?

Step 1: A Sentence of Desire
May I suggest that the first step is choosing music to support you

through the sigil creation process? This is optional of course, but using music, especially music designed to support our creative process and higher consciousness, such as the music of ShapeshifterDNA from Visionary Music, can be a huge support throughout the process. Have it playing in the background as you work.

Sigils are meant to be precise and specific. Brevity is key. I'd like to share a story about a friend who wanted a blanket to put on an altar table. She put it out there to the universe, and the very next morning on her doorstep were left several blankets. However, they were crocheted and looked like someone's grandma made them. They didn't really fit because she hadn't been clear enough about what she wanted. This happens to us all the time. We need to really focus before we put our intent out there... it is what capturing essence is all about.

In creating our sigils, we first start with a sentence that captures the essence of what we want. The sentence must be concise, using just enough words to express the meaning and no more. It should also be created from positive statements. In other words, if your intent is to stop fighting with a loved one, then you wouldn't want your statement to be I WILL NOT FIGHT WITH MY MOTHER. Instead, it should be phrased as I HAVE PEACEFUL RELATIONS WITH MY MOTHER. For this presentation, we will work with: I WANT TO RECEIVE BETTER GUIDANCE SO I KNOW WHAT TO DO NEXT.

This statement doesn't quite capture the essence of the desire. So we alter it. It might therefore become I RECEIVE CLEAR GUIDANCE. In this way, we eliminated the ambiguity of "better than what?" and the concept of one thing being better than another. We eliminate the idea of wanting which implies lack of fulfillment. And finally, we lose the wordiness of "so I know what to do next." We now have a clear statement that captures the essence of our desire.

STEP 2: COMBINING

This next step reminds me of simplifying algebraic statements in which we combine like terms. But don't worry. It isn't nearly so complicated! It's simple. We just take our statement and cross out any repeating letters. Any letter appearing more than once is crossed out and only the remaining letters become part of our new "statement". So take the statement you created in Step 1 and cross out any repeating letters. Rewrite what you have left as your new "statement".

Create your statement:
I RECEIVE CLEAR GUIDANCE
Cross out any repeating letters:
I RECxxVx xLxAx GUxDxNxx
Work with what remains in step three:
I RECV LA GUDN

STEP 3: THE GLYPH

We are now ready to get artistic! We'll combine the remaining letters together overlaying, overlapping, or linking them in the desired manner. You can see from the example that there are lots of possibilities. Rework it, refining and simplifying, until you are completely satisfied with the result.

It should be neither too simplistic nor overly complicated. Think "elegance" with visual appeal. Try several different designs until you hit upon one that resonates with your whole being. At this point, it becomes something much more and beyond the thoughts that created it. And as you work with it, your mind will be programming itself with the command within, and the music playing in the background will amplify this programming on multidimensional levels. Think of it as magnetizing yourself, expanding your magnetic field to draw in what you want.

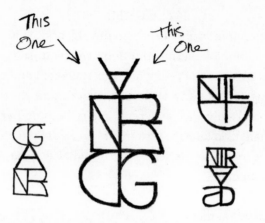

Drawing a shape around the final figure is an optional practice, a sort of protective shell or containment vessel. So play with that as well. Once you have your final version, throw everything else away.

So, take some time now, with your music playing, and get playful with your "statement".

STEP 4: IMPLANTING

Now we have our sigil! It is already being implanted in your subconscious, but let's talk more about ways of enhancing this. As we've already mentioned, use the MUSIC!!! Well-chosen music will assist you in reaching a meditative state; and at that point, the sigil will be introduced to the deep mind. Spare used the phrase, "Drink it in to the mind." This is an excellent metaphor for the process. But don't stop there! The sigil is a power-packed frequency packet. Drink it in to every cell of your being on every single dimension to which you currently have access. Meditate with this idea of the sigil becoming a part of you. You don't need to "try" here. As Spare also wrote, "The magician doesn't charge the sigil, the sigil charges the magician!" It isn't about doing per se, or understanding or knowing if it is happening or not. Know it IS happening. Don't obsess; let the sigil work for you.

For those of you who are frequently challenged by doubt, then try dancing, drumming, or some other mind-stopping physical exertion here as you work with your sigil. Another method shared by Spare, which incorporates our earlier mirror work, is to write the sigil on a mirror and then practice gazing beyond the sigil to your image beneath it in the glass.

Step 5: Let It Go

The next step is to just let it go. The effort has been made, the intent set. Now forget and release the meaning of the sigil completely. Offer it up. You can do this with the music, through reciting mantras, dancing, and/or drumming all with the intent of releasing. Don't expend unnecessary energy for several hours after designing and implanting your sigil either. Just return to everyday activity. You might even want to take a nice nap. In the days ahead, don't talk about it with others. Hold it close to you. Don't do any other meditations either or return to thoughts of the sigil and its meaning.

There is some controversy over whether a sigil should be destroyed or not once it is charged and implanted. That is entirely up to you. I like to hang mine up or place them in a wallet or drawer where I will occasionally be reminded of my intent. That is not to say that I remember what the statement was that helped me create the sigil. It is best to forget that and let the sigil hold all the meaning away from the mind.

Ways to Use your Sigil

There are many ways to approach a sigil. You can write it using colored sands and then let the wind or sea sweep it away. You can create sculpted sigils out of clay and then pound them out of shape back into nothing. Carve into a candle and watch it burn away when you light it or carve it into soap and wash yourself with it as it dissolves from one plane of existence into another. Write it in chalk on the sidewalk or write it on the body... like that scene from *What the Bleep* when Marlee writes all over herself in the tub. Write it on the mirror after a hot shower and let it evaporate. You can also return to listen to the music with which you created your sigil as it now contains all that information regarding your intent.

USING SIGILS RESPONSIBLY

I hardly think I need to add this here, but a reminder never hurts. Sigils should never be used with mal-intent. The application of such magic should only be used with the highest of intentions. We never impose our will on the will of another. We merely co-create for the best of all involved. Nor do we want our will to override the will of higher intelligence. We leave space for something even better than we could have envisioned, trusting in the greater good.

Nor do sigils need to be employed solely for personal gain. Sigils can be created for the healing of our earth, for the purification of our food and water, for the atonement of great wrongs, or for the cultivation of qualities that can assist us on our path such as forgiveness, balance, or compassion. The possibilities are limitless.

In your journal, begin your own sigil-making process. Record your thoughts and feelings through each step. How do you plan on working with your sigil? Have you discovered a way to alter the instructions to better suit your own needs?

THE 4TH GATE

ATTUNEMENT

Together we stand in the River of Words, delighting in the darting little syllables that playfully nibble our toes. Wonder and Splendor are a hardy breed that swim upstream against the current of the Hum Drums and Woes. Cast your net and catch big, fat fish that reflect the radiance of heaven. Throw the small and petty ones back, for all manner of magic resides within. All things become possible when we learn to bait the hook with our careful intent. Let's fry up a bounty of words and let none on the table without our consent.

WORDS

Words were originally intended to be tools for us to master. But at some point in our evolution, everything got turned upside-down and words became our masters. Rather than defining these symbols for ourselves, we inherited the definitions put forth by our ancestors. What's even worse, these symbols became corrupted through misuse, manipulation, and out-and-out lies. A child being beaten by a parent heard "I love you". The politician whose actions repeatedly ignored the unconstitutional nature of new laws pledged "justice for all". People more concerned with their own rights than anyone else's gave lip service to "equal rights". In this age, our lack of consciousness around words is so great that when we are fed an endless diet of lies, we eat them without complaint. When we reawaken to the power of words, we'll awaken to our responsibilities as creators.

~The Unknown Mother

Words are the building blocks of our reality. In *The Unknown Mother*, Wrenne learns, for example, that adjectives link us to our inner judge which either discerns impeccably or separates us from aspects of ourselves. Nouns are labels that perpetuate the illusion of the separate and real. Verbs are our link to "being" in the world. The architecture of a word is enough to invoke its energy. Of all the gates, this one is the most in danger of being "set upon" by the ego. But in a way, it is also a homeopathic remedy. We are using words to free ourselves of the prison of words. So be vigilant as you work.

PRACTICE ONE

As for me, I'd like to do away with should. *What a nasty word! It immediately brings to mind I'm bad because I'm not meeting some expectation... or someone else is bad because they aren't meeting my expectations.*

~*The Unknown Mother*

I once told a new friend I'd just made that he was just like family. I was surprised when his face fell. To me, telling him he was like family meant I felt very comfortable in his presence, that I enjoyed our easy laughter and silliness. He had a totally different concept of the word, having grown up in a situation quite different from mine. He was estranged from a family he couldn't relate to. "Family" was a negatively charged word for him. We had to talk about it in order for my compliment to be taken as such.

Start a "corrupted and reclaimed symbol" journal. Consider words that trigger you. Some of the most universally triggering words are sex, money, God, work, and love, so feel free to start there. Very often, these words are labels that were used to identify us as being "less than", so consider descriptors that may have been applied to you. Work with each word that triggers you and clean it up until you no longer have an emotional, physical or mental reaction to it.

I recently taught a workshop and addressed the group as "you guys". This was met with a strong reaction from two of the women in the group who pointed out to me that they didn't appreciate being called "guys". The rest of the group, also women, had no issue with the word. It led to an interesting conversation. For some of us, "guys" is just a word. It holds no power. For others, "guys" is a masculine word that can be considered disrespectful of women. I was happy to honor the request not to refer to the group as "guys", but I also felt it my duty to help these two women see how their freedom was ensnared by a word.

This is a practice. You don't need to clean every word all at once before proceeding. Expect to return to this after periods of time as new triggers surface.

PRACTICE TWO

NEWS FASTING

One technique that I am asking you to engage at this gate is a "news fast". No newspapers, no TV, no radio news. No *Daily Show* either (sorry Jon). Completely free yourself from the mental stimulus of current events. Don't even engage in conversation about it with others. You can't control whether or not you hear something, but you can control whether or not it takes your attention. You don't have to stop watching things you enjoy, but at least be aware of what you are ingesting. Naturally, over time on your healing path, your tastes will begin to mature, and you won't miss the "junk food" as much. In fact, it will begin to taste like the poison it is. What's the nutritional value of the language you are hearing? Are you watching a drama in which people are slinging insults and angry words back and forth? Why would you want to eat that? Or are you watching the news and getting all fired up about the latest political scandal? As you practice this, don't judge yourself for glancing at an intriguing headline or breaking your fast due to some major historical event. This isn't an exercise is self-judgment. Just do your best. And see if you can let go the need to know and the need to know more. Even if something seems really crucial or important, can you let it go? Be sure to consider in hindsight whether or not knowing whatever information was out there was a matter of life or death, or if it would merely have served to fill you with fear, indignation, or hopelessness. Did you manage without? Did it affect your relationships and interactions with others? What else did you suddenly have time for?

How do you feel going into such a fast? Is there any resistance? Once completed, how did you do on your fast? Was it difficult? Easy? What did you discover about yourself? How did you feel?

PRACTICE THREE

Practice silence. You decide when and where, for how long, and whether or not to allow exceptions.

Write down your plan. When you have implemented it, return and write about how you did. What did you learn? What did you notice in how others responded? How did it feel?

PRACTICE FOUR

Celebrate Thanksgiving today! Express gratitude for all the blessings in your life. Be generous with those you love by offering words of encouragement and thanks. Be generous with yourself by showering yourself with kind thoughts and sweet expressions. Notice what language inspires you. Open up to receive the beauty of language. For example, read poetry that stirs your heart such as Rumi or Rilke. You can even express gratitude for things that haven't happened yet... things you desire... as if they've already happened, dreaming as big as you dare.

Fill a page in your journal with sweet nothings to yourself. You can write in the first or second person. See what resonates. Then start a gratitude section in your journal. Turn to it daily to record at least three things for which you are feeling grateful.

PRACTICE FIVE

In Part II of *The Unknown Mother*, Matrina gives us a deeper look into various parts of speech including prepositions:

Prepositions are words that answer when, where, at what time, and those kinds of details – without for example. Does that word hold an emotional charge for you?... There are other gems hiding within other prepositions. How about according to? How often have you given away your personal power or better judgment to some other authority? And against is a power-packed unit of meaning. What are you against? Who is against you? Throughout *tends to hold a lot of personal history energy in it, as in "throughout my life, this has been the case".*

~*The Unknown Mother*

Here is a list of prepositions should you choose to do the exercise she suggested of investigating any connections you have or make unconsciously with these words. Just focus on ones that stand out. Remember, you're simply drawing energy out of these little units of meaning by freely associating. Just get curious and see what comes up.

About	Beside	On
Above	Between	Onto
According to	Beyond	On top of
After	Despite	Out of
Against	During	Outside
Along	Except	Over
Alongside	From	Past
Amid	In addition to	Since
Among	In back of	Through
Apart from	In front of	Throughout
Around	Inside	Towards
Away from	In spite of	Under
Because of	Instead of	Until
Before	Into	Up
Behind	Like	With
Below	Near	Within
Beneath	Off	Without

PRACTICE SIX

YES AND NO

Why is it so darn hard for so many of us to say "No"?

It fills us with dread when we have to turn someone or

something down. We may even enter avoidance mode just so we don't have to say those two little letters. Even if we've made a commitment to ourselves to get better at saying "No", we often get stuck in the energy drain of having to explain ourselves. Does it have to be so hard? No! In fact, starting now, you can make a decision to just say no.

First we have to decide that "No" is a complete sentence. It need not be followed by a conversation, internal or otherwise, that makes us question our choice. Next, we seek opportunities to practice. When someone makes a request of us, and we genuinely have no interest in it, simply say "No." Not "No, thank you anyway, but you see, I have to wash my hair." Not "No, I can't work overtime this week because my kids are sick." Not "No, I can't organize your fundraiser. I'm so sorry. I'm just so busy." Not "No, I can't bake a dozen cookies for the party because, because, because..." No apologies. No excuses.

Let "No" be free of justification. Of course, the temptation to explain will be strong. The other person will be waiting for your excuse; it's our habit and our expectation. But watch what happens when you don't give it. You might be surprised to find that nothing happens. Or if he or she should press, decide that you will simply smile and say "No" again. If you want to share your reason, then do so, but not because you feel you need an excuse. Do it because you truly want to share the information.

Of course, if we've been a "Yes" person, suddenly saying "No" can really stir things up. Suddenly, we're not as agreeable in the eyes of others used to getting their way. What a great opportunity to stand in your power and restate your "No." Whatever this person may throw at you, whatever manipulations have worked in the past to get you to cave, decide that you will stand firm. Imagine yourself in a protective bubble that is impenetrable to such tactics. Feel the joy of proclaiming your healthy boundary. Feel the joy of self-approval!

Then again, maybe the trouble isn't saying no so much as

saying yes to the things we really want. Maybe we hold some belief that, in taking for ourselves, we are preventing someone else from having what they want. Maybe we're afraid to suddenly get what we secretly desire because we're sure we don't deserve it. Whatever the reason, maybe it's time to short circuit this withholding from self. Practicing saying yes is a great exercise to strengthen our receiving muscle.

Think back to times when you really wanted to say yes to something but didn't. What were you afraid of? Who would it hurt? Do you regret your choice? Did you say no to something you wanted because you felt you had to say yes to something you didn't?

Now think of some things you really want for yourself today. Practice saying "Yes" to fully receiving each of these things. Practice in front of a mirror or with a sympathetic friend. Don't just say the word, feel the energy of Yes!

"Yes, I accept healthy, balanced relationships with others in my life now."

"Yes, I accept a day all to myself to nurture me."

"Yes, I accept that you want to treat me to dinner."

What does it feel like to allow yourself to say "Yes!"? Really, it is all life asks of us in any moment. Life just wants us to open our arms to experience everything it has to offer. From this place of accepting what comes, then we are free to decide what works for us and what doesn't. We are once again free to say no.

These two simple words are so important to our well-being. They are enough to chart our course in Life. When we have easy access to both of them, we make choices that help us align with our Truth and our desire. When we learn to use them without hesitation, we stop wasting energy that can be put to better use.

So make a decision today to start playing with yes and no. Begin by noticing occasions when you use them. Then begin noticing the times when you are saying the one you don't really mean. Just a little bit of awareness will open up a window of opportunity for you to walk through the next time you are poised on the edge of a yes or a no. Your automatic or fear-based response will soon be preceded by a breath of space in which you can choose a new course of action. In time, yes and no will flow from your lips with complete conviction and ease.

PRACTICE SEVEN

MORE TRIGGERS

In your journal, take some time to consider the following highly charged words or phrases. When do you find yourself using them? When others use them, what do you notice?

- Must
- Have to
- Should
- What if...
- Always
- Never
- Can't

PRACTICE EIGHT

One of my favorite poets, Kirk Nugent, has said that the two most important words in our language are "I AM". They certainly are important. This phrase declares our state of being, packing a powerful punch. But is the "punch" black magic, followed by derogatory terms and self-demeaning description, or is it white magic, affirmative and life-giving? Turn your attention to this phrase and notice what happens when you or others use it. What happens if you use it with more conscious attention?

THE 5TH GATE

ATTUNEMENT

Some are weavers and others spiders. Which, dear reader, are you? Would you like some sanity in a world full of spiders? What is one to do? Do you design a cloth of many colors that inspires and uplifts? Or do you cast a sticky web that hooks and trips? Armed with a gilded New World dictionary, let us become master artisans, creating blankets that comfort and soothe, until we become our own best friends. Write no more yourself into a victim role. Claim your True Voice and free your soul!

Storytelling

We've all been writing fairytales since we were born. Your life has been a fairytale, filled with dark and foreboding characters, fairy godmothers, magical animals, princes, and princesses... And they really do come true. Look around you. Everything you see, the people in your life, the objects – they are the direct result of your fairytale writing. Let me tell you a secret... If we could just change our stories, make them kinder, gentler – more benign, at least – the world would change.

~The Unknown Mother

Now that we have a deeper understanding of both letters and words and the energies they carry, we are ready to string them together meaningfully in ways that inspire, encourage, enlighten, and entertain rather than demean, frighten, discourage, and depress. The 5th Gate is about the stories we tell and hear and how we can learn to become better storytellers. We come to recognize that the way we've been telling our stories hasn't always served us. In fact, we've often written ourselves into tight corners and small boxes, assuming the role of victim or perpetrator, forgetting that we can just as easily be the heroes and heroines. It's all in the telling.

Practice One

Let's start with the concept of incongruence or what happens when what we feel or mean and what we actually say is not aligned. It is often indicated through our physiology. We get a niggling feeling in our gut or our brow knits together after having expressed ourselves. Perhaps we are afraid of hurting someone's feelings, or we feel the pressure to respond in a certain way.

In what ways are you incongruent with your speech? Watch

for it and learn to catch yourself. Take a look at what image you are trying to protect. Is it worth the energy? Also realize that just because you are exhibiting conflict through your physiology doesn't mean your physiology is to be trusted. You may just be moving out of a deeply entrenched habit with your mind well ahead of your body. Incongruence helps point our awareness towards imbalance, but it alone does not discern the root of the imbalance.

Spend some time with these thoughts and your journal.

PRACTICE TWO

The Toltec have a wonderful word to describe all of the voices inside our heads that are constantly commenting on everything we do, think, and feel: a *mitote* is a marketplace, a busy, bustling center of activity with plenty to distract us, tempt us, and confuse us. We all have a mitote in our heads; and until we can hear it from the perception of the objective witness, it can control our thoughts and, ultimately, the decisions we make.

Begin to identify all of the "people" in your mitote. These are the voices in your head that are constantly vying for your attention. Typically, they are not a helpful crowd. Do you have an inner saboteur who frequently says things like "You can't possibly do that, so why even try?" Or maybe you have a loud inner victim that is always placing blame and crying "Why me?" Some other possibilities include the Judge, the Queen, the Prostitute, the Hero, and the Wounded Child. A great resource for determining which archetypes operate the stalls of your mitote is *Sacred Contracts* by Caroline Myss.

Write your discoveries and insights in your journal.

PRACTICE THREE

I remember once approaching one of my Toltec teachers at a Circle of Fire event; I asked, "Can I bother you?" He responded, "No, you can't bother me, but you can ask me a question." I will never forget that! Of course, the underlying agreement I carried was that I was a pest, an intrusion whenever I needed something. This teacher helped me wake up to myself – I had fallen under the spell of my own assumption. He also modeled so beautifully a boundary that so many of us ignore. None of us want to be bothered. So why would we ever say "yes" to such a question? And further still, why would we consider anyone who approaches us a bother in the first place. It was a beautiful lesson in habitual assumption making.

Which reminds me of a time not long after this when I was taking a homeowner's class, and an insurance person came to speak to us. Whenever he addressed one of the women, he would call us "pretty little lady". I suppose he felt he was being complimentary, but it turned my stomach and felt so demeaning. Granted, I had to take responsibility for the charge I felt, but at the same time, if he was interested in his own development, it would have been a good idea for him to look at why he was using that phrase and what beliefs were underlying it... judgments that seeped out every time he said it. He also had the habit of saying, "I'm going to pick on you," every time he used someone as an example to illustrate a point. I just kept thinking of my experience with my teacher and wanted to say, "You don't need to pick on us, Mister; just ask your question."

How does your language reflect the assumption you make? What spells have you been casting? What phrases do you use that may be alienating other people?

PRACTICE FOUR

Gossip. It means different things to different people. I've heard many people express that they wouldn't have anything to talk about if they couldn't gossip. I've heard others uphold it as a value... a cherished way to connect and share information. Well, for our purposes, let's decide neither of those justifications is true.

Gossip is basically talking cheap, a form of "black magic". It isn't just about sharing information, because most of the information we gossip about no one really needs to know. It is instead an energy drain that serves no real purpose, other than to undermine others or even ourselves. It is by and large a form of entertainment for those with nothing better to do and no better way to relate to others.

In *The Unknown Mother*, Matrina and Wrenne overhear a very distasteful gossip session in the grocery store. Spend a week keeping track of your participation in gossip or simply observe others engaged in it. What do you notice about your energy and the energy of those so engaged? How have you "bought into" the gossip of others?

If you want, decide to abstain from gossiping for a period of time. What happens when you have a juicy tidbit but refrain from sharing it? In what new ways are you relating to others as you abstain? How are others reacting to you?

In what ways do you gossip about yourself? Do you demean yourself either in your own mind or in conversations with others with phrases like "I can't do that", or "I'm such an idiot!"? Why do these tapes run? Pay attention and become aware of the spells you are casting. With some effort, you can turn that ol' black magic into self-respect and love.

Write any responses in your journal.

PRACTICE FIVE

NEW WORLD DICTIONARY

In *The Unknown Mother*, Matrina challenges Wrenne to rewrite the dictionary. She explains:

Faith is stored in words. You need only listen to someone speak to know where his faith lies... A New World dictionary is a necessity because we are entering a new world. As I've mentioned before, certain words and symbols are becoming obsolete. As creators, it's crucial that we pull our faith out of old concepts and place in them in redefined ones.

~The Unknown Mother

Create a new world dictionary. To give you an example, for years I felt that rejection was something that said everything about me. It was painful to feel rejected. I knew the word didn't have nearly as much power over me as I was giving it, so I redefined it. Now, rejection means: an indication from the universe that something better is coming; a gentle nudge that says, "Not this way, Beloved."

Redefine the words in your "corrupted and reclaimed symbol" entries that you started in Gate 4, Practice One. Whenever a word pops up in daily life that you wish to redefine, add it to your journal.

PRACTICE SIX

TELLING OUR STORIES A NEW WAY

I remember a day my mother called to tell me my father was in the hospital. She gave me a second by second play of the day before rather than telling me the most essential information up front. With each word, I became more and more agitated waiting for the point. Was he going to live or not?! It seemed to me she should have started with that tidbit and then told me the rest of the backstory.

What do you consider to be communication faux pas? In what way do you manipulate the emotions of others by holding back, over-drama-tizing, or pretending to be more upbeat? Do you ever over-explain or justify your position? Do you lack an economy of words saying more than necessary? Do you ever fake a voice quality? Do you get tongue-tied? In what situations?

REWRITING OUR STORIES

Matrina suggests rewriting the stories we tell about our lives. These fairytales don't have to make sense to anyone but you. They can be sewn together with bits of dreams, real experiences, poetry, and surrealism. The important thing is that they honor a deeper truth than traditional fairy tales and point you in the direction of your authentic power. There are no victims here, so take pleasure in your crafting.

Consider how often you exaggerate the truth or downplay things to make yourself look better. Do you leave important little details out or make excuses for how you handled things? Do you attempt to make others look like they are at fault? If you do these things to control how others perceive you, then there is some self-judgment going on and, likely, a bit of denial. Is it really worth the energy you're putting out to sustain some idea of image? But if you choose to tell your stories to make a difference in how **you** perceive **yourself**, if you cut the judgment and learn from your mistakes, you can become the hero of your own story.

We are storytellers. And once told, our stories come to life. So become the master of your stories, taking what was once a scary scene and shedding new light into its dark corners. You will look at stories of image, life, love, money, work, career, religion, fear, courage… and you will choose to tell them in a new way. Turn your tales of woe into tales of power and your tales of power into actual power.

Here is an example of a story I used to tell. I hope for your sake it doesn't sound too familiar:

The Original Story

Will I ever be happy? I swear, just when I think I've had a spiritual revelation, I end up back here feeling small and powerless. I just don't think I'll ever be different. What if my nervous system is beyond repair? What if I'm hardwired to be an anxious mess the rest of my life? I just can't take it. What has this whole journey been for, anyway? I've spent thousands of dollars and for what? I'm still me. I'm still resentful, still scared and still confused. What am I even here for?

Now here's that same story after I rewrote it as a tale of power. Notice the difference and use it as inspiration for your own tales:

The Rewrite
I want to know what it is to be happy, thought the young woman to herself. What will it take for me to reprogram my nervous system, to clean it out and charge it with the forces of Acceptance, Forgiveness, and Love?

She decided that she would look directly at what hurts. If she felt lonely, she would look at that. If she felt judgmental, she would look at that. No matter how difficult, she would face what was making her unhappy with a warrior's heart, listening to the voice without giving in to it.

The voice was ugly. It said that she wasn't good enough. It revealed her prejudices and shortcomings. It cried that she deserved better. It whimpered that no one liked her or cared about her. It made preferences. It told such big lies... and many little ones like things are fixed and can't change for the better, or that someone is bound to notice, take pity on her, and rescue her if she would only look desperate enough.

Sometimes, the fear was very convincing. But each time, the woman would state, "This is not me; I refuse to identify with it. This is not what I want anymore." She challenged the lies again and again. Whenever a feeling came from confusion, resentment, desperation, or resistance, the woman stated her desire to be free and stated her intent for new feelings of love to enter. These new feelings were like tender flowers in the snow, and she nurtured and encouraged them as slight as they felt.

In time, these flowers were blooming like a garden in the springtime. They were sweet and colorful, just like the happiness that now claimed the woman's nervous system. And it only went to follow that the woman changed in many ways on the outside too. She walked with more grace, she was patient, at peace. There was a femininity, a softness, about her that wasn't there before. She was very powerful, her faith intact and her intent clean and sharp. Love, courage, beauty, freedom. This is what she brought with her as she entered any room.

Here is another story I used to tell, this one about finding true love:

The Original Story

I was so in love with Javier. He knew how I felt about him. How could he be so cavalier with my feelings? He didn't even bother to tell me that he started dating someone else. I had to find out and feel like a complete and utter idiot. Why didn't he choose me? What's wrong with me? Will anyone ever love me? Will anyone ever choose me?

And here is the rewrite. Not a sappy, happy tale, but one that empowers me to live free of expectations that would otherwise rob me of my sanity.

The Rewrite

On a gloriously crisp day full of the light of the sun, a young woman decided to venture out of her high tower and into the world of men. She was timid as she had heard terrible, loathsome things about this world, and even, in fact, experienced some of them. But she was also courageous because she sought other beings with which to play. She wanted to have fun.

She came upon a gathering of like-minded individuals who honored learning and spiritual growth. And as she approached this circle, a young man appeared. His eyes were drunk with love. "You are a beautiful woman," he said. "And you are a beautiful man," said she. They embraced and radiated pure love and light that anyone within a certain radius could feel and share in, in full joy of each other's company, with no expectations, no stories, no attachments.

But a moment came when she asked, "Is this possible? Can I be so in love with life? Can this really be a man who is secure in who he is, does not insult me when I go against him, does not plead when I need my space, lives his own life and does not cower in jealousy when I express love towards another? Will he erase the wrongs done, be there for me when I need him, and treat me like a goddess?"

Is this possible, he asked himself. Have I found a woman who allows me my own dream? Is she truly comfortable with silence? Is she the ruthlessly compassionate warrior goddess she appears to be? Will she be faithful to me, tend the wounds I've carried, and allow me to be the king I was born to be?

Probably not, they thought. So they remained in an embrace just happy to enjoy one another's presence in the Now. And both lived happily ever after because neither needed the other to be happy.

Your tales don't have to be sugarcoated. They can be gritty and real. Yet the hero or heroine should always triumph. They'll help you to remember that you are much bigger than your problems and petty issues.

It's time to rewrite your own stories. Choose one from your past that you often retell in which you have always played the role of victim. Rewrite it in your journal in such a way as to bring to light the true gifts of the experience. Turn cruelty into kindness. Turn loss into triumph. Don't stop there. Also journal about how it felt to go through this process with your story. Notice where you might be in resistance to stepping out of blame or guilt. No need to judge yourself. Just notice. Then write a different story about that! Add more stories as you feel inspired to do so.

THE 6TH GATE

ATTUNEMENT

Stop. Wait. Don't do a thing. Capture that moment of nothing from which all ideas sing. Pay too much attention, and you're sure to go broke, so allow life to carry you through that mirror of smoke. Ears open, arms wide, we swim with the tide; we now know the Truth because we hear it inside. When you listen with your bones, you know what is true. And no one can take that away from you.

LISTENING

Music, Spirit, the Great Mystery – whatever you call it – is always speaking to us. Learning to really listen means waking up to this fact and taking in the guidance that is always with us. Then and only then can it also speak through us. Then we can sing without singing.

~The Unknown Mother

It is time to look at how we listen. Really, you've been building your capacity to listen at each gate up to now. So here we are simply bringing our full attention to it. I consider listening to be an art... as much as creating music or dance. Not everyone has developed their musical or movement abilities, and it is the same with listening. We listen with our ears, yes, but we can also listen with our bones and every other fiber of our being. We can even listen with our aura. The deeper the listening, the more likely we are to pick up on the messages that lie beneath the surface and between the lines. The deeper the listening, the more we are able to tap into Silent Knowledge, or the clear wisdom that is always available to us in every moment.

Did you know that the words "listen" and "silent" are permutations of each other? There is a reason that meditation is part of so many traditions. Meditation is a form of listening, and it helps us connect with that still, small voice within. It works a muscle that has long since given its authority over to our sense of vision and image. We tend to believe what we see. Listening deeply helps us believe what we hear... or not.

Some things to ponder in your journal: the sense of listening is one of the first to develop prenatally and one of the last senses to leave us when we die. Wouldn't you say that implies a certain significance in the importance of being able to hear? We are bombarded with sound even from before the time we are born. Do we ever stop to consider the effects this sound is having on our bodies, minds, and spirits?

PRACTICE ONE

The following practice will assist you in opening the ear chakras. You may want to create a recording as a guided visualization for yourself until you learn the process or do it with a friend, taking turns.

Begin with the breath. Release and relax. Be still and relax some more. Now listen. Attend to external sounds. Attend to internal sounds. Allow your imagination to fulfill your hearing. Listen. Attend to what you cannot hear. Relax some more. Allow your ears to open as if yawning. Now hear the many voices. Now hear everything at once... the grand orchestration. Create with it. Play with it. Hum and sound. Sit in complete stillness. Now turn your attention inside out. Be heard. Allow the Composer to listen to you.

Do nothing.

After several minutes, record your thoughts and experience.

PRACTICE TWO

Sound isn't processed through the mind, as are stimuli through our other senses. The vibration of sound impacts the body immediately. In fact, we don't only hear through our ears. Our entire bodies are resonance chambers; our very bones are perceptive of and receptive to vibration. To believe we hear only with our ears – or sing only with our voice boxes for that matter – limits not only our experience, but our ability as well. It makes us even more vulnerable to the force of entrainment.

~The Unknown Mother

We don't just hear with our ears. We hear with our entire bodies; it is a very sensitive instrument. In addition, we don't just hear sounds in our environment. In some Eastern traditions, they are aware of several levels of hearing, as mentioned previously:

- Vaikhari or coarse sounds we hear with our ears
- Madhyama or mental sounds – the voices in our heads
- Pashyanti or dream sounds
- Para or transcendent sounds beyond the senses

With your ear chakras open, begin to pay attention to all of your environments from the point of view of your ears. Notice the difference from one environment to the next. What does work sound like? What does home sound like? What do different rooms in your home sound like? What does an environment of fun sound like? What does church sound like? What does your backyard sound like? Which environments bring pleasure to your ears and which bring discomfort or even pain?

Now shift your perspective and pay attention from the point of view of your entire body as a listening organ. What changes does this shift bring about?

Take your listening deeper. Pay attention to environments in which music is playing in the background. Perhaps you are at a restaurant or shopping. What impact is this music having on your mood, thoughts, energy? Does it seem to fit or contradict the environment? Is it too loud? Too quiet? Do you notice people responding to it in any way? Are there other sources of noise competing with it?

Now consider, as you sit quietly, each of the levels of hearing. Allow yourself to dream about them, freely associating as you tune into a new, deeper form of listening.

Record your responses and discoveries in your journal.

PRACTICE THREE

In *The Unknown Mother*, Matrina helps Wrenne listen through a mechanic's speech, who has told Wrenne she needs expensive repairs, into the truth:

You know when something resonates with you or not. When we only hear the surface value of sounds or even words, we're missing so much of what's being said on subtler levels. We deny our intuition.

By becoming better listeners and not just hearing what we want or expect to hear, we build our "lie detection" muscles. Let's do some muscle-building now.

BODY LANGUAGE

Notice either by observing others or witnessing in yourself the distance or closeness a speaker maintains to his audience. Is there eye contact? Gestures? Too many? Is the body rigid or fluid? What kinds of gestures or stances make you uncomfortable? Is the listener present or a million miles away? Does that seem to make a difference to the speaker or not?

LISTENING FOR INTENTIONS

Spend a day noticing how the voice reveals emotions, thoughts and feelings as you listen to others either on TV or radio or in person. What might be driving their communication? Need? Fear? Love? Information? As you listen more deeply, you will also come to listen more deeply to yourself.

MIXED MESSAGES

Remember incongruence? Consider the following phrase, "Oh, I love your new haircut." Try saying this phrase in different ways, playfully attaching different emotional qualities, and notice how it feels and sounds. What do you notice in the voice that is afraid? That is insincere? That is angry? That is genuine?

Write about anything you observed while considering these questions.

PRACTICE FOUR

My friends at Visionary Music, creators of Quantum Entrainment

Sonic Therapy (QEST), have been teaching their listening technique called *Become the Music* for a very long time. They have a flash movie you can watch that helps to describe the process:

> *Mastering this technique while listening to our music will enhance and amplify the benefits you will receive tenfold. Use this technique to enhance your DNA Activation process, deepen meditations and enhance your shamanic journeying skills.*

This practice can also deepen your listening skills, especially in being able to listen with your whole being... not just your ears.

Part 1: http://youtu.be/Qn0tyx2GYZY
Part 2: http://youtu.be/FZqlQj6-TWU

After watching these videos, write about your experience in your journal. How did it feel to become the music? Did it come naturally or do you feel like you need more practice?

Practice Five

Vocal Qualities

Consider the kinds of expressive habits you find off-putting. Perhaps you cringe when someone is nasal sounding or too loud. What if someone is too quiet or unintelligible? Hostile? Do they ever get to the point? Do they speak too fast or too slow? Do they say way more than necessary or repeat themselves over and over? Do you?

Also consider the kinds of vocal qualities you find most attractive. Perhaps you like a sexy, breathy voice. Do you respect people more if they look you in the eye? We're simply building awareness with this exercise. It isn't about right and wrong. We're noticing, discerning, and simply taking notes.

Record your findings and thoughts in your journal.

PRACTICE SIX

WORKING WITH AFFIRMATIONS

Words hold energy. We can use this energy for better or worse. Many people know of and have tried using affirmations or positive statements designed to change a negative thought pattern. I myself, having been exposed to the wonderful teachings of Abraham Hicks and others, have tried them. Sometimes, they work and sometimes, well... they don't do much. Sometimes our conflicting beliefs are just too strong.

I began a new practice with affirmations awhile back when I started to understand more of the "secret" relationship between our words, our thoughts, and sound, and the hidden power and interplay of each. The practice arose spontaneously during a meditation, and it has had a much greater impact than any affirmation practice I have had.

It's very easy but does take effort and a willingness to sound and feel ridiculous at first. Take any affirmation. Examples include, "I am centered and peaceful" or "My life is filled with abundance." The cool thing with this particular practice is that you really don't have to pretend to believe something you don't. You don't have to think yourself through it either. All you have to do is be willing to say it. The "secret" aspects of word, thought, and sound will take care of the rest.

Now, sit yourself down in a quiet place where you will not be disturbed. If you can be in front of a mirror to witness yourself, all the better. Begin to say your chosen affirmation. If it sounds phony to you, then say it that way, with all the sarcasm you can muster. If you want to sing it, sing it. If nothing comes up but a gurgle, that's perfect too. The idea is to say it in as many ways as possible feeling for the moments of resonance when parts or all of the statement ring true. Keep at it. It may not happen right away. This is the practice of transmuting energy. Persist. Play. Get your body involved. Shake. Wiggle. Get up and stomp.

Allow the practice to reveal to you just where your blocks are. It will happen. You may even have a release as you move through resistance and longing into the place where you can sense the truth of your statement that was really there all along.

As you open and express, you will come to the point where all the resistance drops away. And there, you will find yourself hearing the words of your affirmation as if for the first time. You will start to state the affirmation without the theatrics, drama, and playfulness. Go slowly here. You will begin to speak each word with its own weight and sincerity. Again, tears may flow. You will begin to feel the truth of the statement in different areas of your body. You will sense joy arising. And you will empower yourself.

Spend some time recording how this process went for you in your journal. What did you learn about yourself?

THE 7TH GATE

ATTUNEMENT

Everything vibrates. Everything sings. Everything moves. And everything rings. When you get close to the song of another, something quite natural begins to take over. We enter a dance and a give and take, and how this is done is the beauty we make.

VIBRATION

As we resonate with the higher frequencies of love, compassion, and equanimity, we learn to radiate these qualities and not absorb everything that crosses our path. Perhaps more importantly, we have to be able to "stop and wait" in order to choose what we entrain to in our day-to-day lives. In terms of offering our services to others, we need to be the stronger force, entraining everyone we meet to better health and well-being.

~The Unknown Mother

Matrina taught Wrenne about two scientific terms having to do with Sound Healing, resonance and entrainment. Resonance, the first term, refers to the frequency at which an object naturally vibrates. Frequency, by the way, is the number of vibrations per second with higher pitches vibrating more rapidly. Resonance is natural. When we say things like "I resonate with that", we mean we are aligned with it, in tune, or in agreement. Like resonates with like. As an example of resonance, imagine that you live on a busy street and that a very large truck speeds by. When it passes, objects on your shelves rattle slightly. Those objects are resonating. Throughout your week, see if you can identify other examples of resonance in your environment. Maybe you have a sink full of dishes that vibrate when you turn on the garbage disposal. Maybe a picture falls from the wall when you slam a door.

Physiologically speaking, the body is really one big resonator. The vagus nerve, the largest nerve in the body, runs from the ear through the greater portion of the body including most of the internal organs. The ear is made to pick up a wide range of high frequency sounds, but most of what we hear is low... traffic, machines, computers, lights... High frequency sounds replenish the brain and activate the cortex. The ears are said to be among the most important sense organs. The ears control the body's sense of balance and are the conductors of the entire nervous system. Through the medulla, the auditory nerve connects with all the muscles in the body. Your muscle tone, equilibrium, flexibility, and vision, are all affected by sound. Through the vagus nerve, the inner ear connects with the larynx, heart, lungs, stomach, liver, bladder, kidneys, small intestine and large intestine.

In terms of sound healing, we are usually working to raise and maintain our frequency. But how is this done?

Our second term will answer that question. Entrainment is the interaction between two closely related rhythmic cycles. They have a mutual influence on one another. Where the motto of resonance is "like attracts like", entrainment is more like "opposites attract". One rhythmic cycle, the stronger force, will usually overcome the weaker one. The most common example of entrainment involves a man named Christiaan Huygens.

Huygens observed the relationship between two pendulum clocks that had come into the same swinging rhythm. When two things are out of phase, small amounts of energy are transferred that set up a negative feedback loop. Think of two people with opposing views trying to have a conversation. One can either convince the other that he is right, thus both individuals move into synchrony. Or they can discuss the issue to such extremes that they move into exact polar opposites of one another, as in complimentary entrainment. Or they can move in a complex and creative dance of seeing each other's point of view, as in harmonic entrainment. To return to the example of the clock, the pendulums can move in completely different rhythms; but given time, they will either move into moments of synchrony, antiphase, or harmonic entrainment. In any case, the period of swing will be exactly the same whether or not the phase is.

It is common for women living together in dorms or other close quarters to begin to menstruate with the same cycle. This is another example of entrainment. If you have ever caught yourself tapping your foot to music, you have been overtaken by entrainment! Similarly, think how breathing slow and steady can bring a racing heart back to pace. Can you think of additional example of entrainment?

It is through the principles of resonance and entrainment that sound affects matter. So, understanding these principles, we begin to understand why sound has such a huge impact on us and our health. Pay attention to your environment throughout the week and see if you can't spot more examples.

Someone at a workshop recently asked me why, if the higher frequency always entrains a lower one, was it so easy for her to get sucked into other people's dramas? It was a great question. It's important to understand that it isn't that the higher frequency will always entrain a lower frequency. Rather, the stronger frequency will entrain the weaker. While we, as conscious beings, are aware we must keep our frequency high and often do, there are still places in us where we resonate with slower, denser vibrations. When we find ourselves getting pulled down by another's heaviness, it isn't the laws of frequency that are at fault, any more than it is the fault of the person vibrating there. We have within us our own weaknesses to deal with, and such a person comes into our life to illuminate the work to be done.

I had another client with newfound healing abilities who found himself getting pulled into the drama of one of his first clients. He wasn't sure what to do. He didn't realize it wasn't his job to entertain his client's sob story. It was his job to resonate at the frequency of her potential, giving her the opportunity to pull herself up out of her story.

Frequency is directly related to intent in that the energy of our thoughts resonates with certain frequencies. If we find ourselves frustrated to bring about the changes we desire in our lives, chances are good that we have not yet learned the lessons frequency teaches: like attracts like. If we spend the majority of our time on the negative, it pulls our energy... or frequency... down and likely away from our hearts' desires.

Building our awareness of our own frequency and cleaning from our systems the habits and beliefs that pull us down is necessary to create the life we want. This entire book contains tools that help us do just that. The following practices will help you develop a deeper awareness of the subtleties of vibration.

PRACTICE ONE

Let's revisit an activity from the 6th Gate. Take note of any music that enters your environment either by your intention or by passive exposure. How is it impacting your mood, emotions, thoughts, physiology? How might it be impacting those around you?

Now take a look at mood. How do the moods of others affect you? How does your mood affect others? Are you able to maintain a happy mood when surrounded by lower vibrations? Do you ever notice that a cheerful friend can lift you out of your bitter moods?

Entrainment is happening everywhere, all of the time. Keep your eyes and ears peeled and record any observations.

PRACTICE TWO

Given the opportunity, expose yourself to new kinds of sound. Listen to music you wouldn't have before. Go to a drum circle. Learn to play the didgeridoo. Notice how these new sounds strike new chords in your awareness of body, mind or spirit.

If you have access to a piano or some other instrument, play just one note. Notice how that one note feels and impacts your body and mind. Close your eyes and really meditate on that one note. Then try another note. What has changed? Where does it resonate? Which do you prefer? Can you compare the same note on two instruments?

Write about your discoveries in your journal.

Practice Three

The science of Cymatics reveals how vibration creates form. It reveals our birth – for we, like the sand, are subject to vibration. Some unseen, unheard song is creating us – singing us into being. We are the sand upon the vibrating plate, taking shape into our existence, believing we are the peaks and points that take form, and believing we are this or that. In reality, we're malleable, moldable, and at the mercy of the Great Sound. For if this great sound were to cease or be disrupted, these mighty houses we've constructed would disperse like so many grains of sand flung to the wind. Something is conscious of us. It listens as it plays upon the instruments that we are. It takes delight in the cacophony, an orchestration so grand it is far beyond our contemplation. It is masterful, elegant, swift, and awesome. It is the Song of the Universe – and more. It is our Composer, and one who loves beyond conditions, beyond the beyond. If the law of "as above, so below" holds true, then we too are composers. We too sing songs that breathe shape into reality. But are we listening? Are we paying attention to the compositions we create?

~The Unknown Mother

When I taught the 6th grade, I did an activity with my class in which we listened to different kinds of music. The kids got to draw on big pieces of paper whatever they were feeling from the music. Time and again, students on opposite sides of the room would have the exact same elements in their pictures inspired by the same piece of music. It was fascinating. Of course, their pictures were also unique. What mysterious force of inspiration is at play here? Could it be related to the way vibration creates form?

Explore the work of Hans Jenny, father of Cymatics. Do a Google search to discover this science and its implications of how sound affects matter. You might also be interested in the work of Masaru Emoto who experimented with the effects of vibration on water; though his science has been called into question, it is still fascinating work.

Now, select a piece of music you love and enter a meditation with it. Imagine you are a droplet of water or the sand upon a Cymatic plate. Feel how the music shifts and reorganizes your cells into geometric designs and shapes. Feel your very blood respond to the vibration of the music.

You might want to do this experiment using colored pencils or crayons to draw a response to the music.

PRACTICE FOUR

Notice the mechanical sounds around you be they the hum of a refrigerator or the whooshing of windshield wipers. Notice how the sound may be impacting your body, mind and spirit. Then begin to gently tone with the noisemaker. Find a pitch that resonates or harmonizes with the washing machine. Create a rhythm that complements the clicking of the copy machine. Be playful, and notice what shifts, if anything.

PRACTICE FIVE

Ever take a wrong turn only to come upon something totally magical? Or maybe you've struck up a conversation with a total stranger and discovered a common friend. Perhaps you've been feeling really down, struggling with some personal issue that is making it difficult for you to see clearly, when a friend posts something online that breaks your heart open and clears the clouds.

As you become more and more aware of how you use your energy, specifically in its relation to language, and you begin to focus that energy in such a way as to ask for and then create the life you desire, be sure to make room for meaningful coincidences...which really are not just coincidences but synchronicities, signs of flow and grace.

There's always a razor's edge to walk, though. Over-interpretation of things and why they happened... when everything becomes a sign that supports an agenda you have... can lead to self-delusion and eventual confusion and heartache. So how can you tell the difference between something meaningful and meaningless when aspects of the ego are so quick to latch on and manufacture meaning? Don't go looking for synchronicity. Let it find you. It unfolds without effort, like a dream.

Some synchronicities, referred to as signs of power, let us know our intent has been heard and answered. There may or may not be outer signs of manifestation, but we still know we have received affirmation. Others attempt to steer us on our path whether by opening doors or placing obstacles before us. Still others are lessons, sometimes difficult, but always beneficial. They can also serve to simply remind us we are really dreaming all of the time... or that we are loved and supported.

What are your beliefs about coincidences and synchronicities? Have you ever experienced a meaningful coincidence? When something synchronous happens to you as you work through the 10 Gates of Sound, write about it in your journal.

PRACTICE SIX

A great way to intentionally work with synchronicity is to create a vision board. A vision board is a canvas filled with images that you love, things that make you smile and bring up positive memories, emotions, or associations. They are collages of things you would love to manifest and experience. You'll need scissors, some glue, and construction paper or cardboard. Grab some old magazines, preferably ones rich with images... not just your typical men's or woman's rag, but ones that focus on extraordinary places, foods, art, animals, etc. Then set aside some time and space to create. Light a candle. Play some music. Flip through your resources and cut out anything that speaks to you, images or text. Try not to censor yourself. Follow your initial impulse. Once you've assembled all your images, begin to arrange them on cardboard or construction paper. When you are happy with your design, glue the images in place. When complete, spend some time really "feeeeling" what each of the images means to you. Then play the "future gratitude" game that was introduced at Gate 4, Practice Four. Finally, hang your vision board where you can see it and enjoy it daily. Now you're ready to receive any synchronicities related to your board in the days, weeks or months ahead.

Record your experience of creating your board and how it felt to feel into each image. Did you change your mind about any images? Why? Also record any effects that arise as a result of having made this for yourself.

THE 8TH GATE

ATTUNEMENT

Everything that has breath was created to sing praise to the source of its existence.

TONING

Toning is an opportunity to communicate across time and dimensions. It transcends left-brain knowing. It's our chance to send out musical messages – vibrational programming – to the many, many parts of ourselves. When we tone, we learn to really listen – to pay attention without breaking the bank, so to speak. Toning is about managing our attention. We learn to contribute our unique expression, with awareness, to the greater whole. As I mentioned before, it's communication beyond words and languages and the divisions they create. Toning is universal.

~The Unknown Mother

From Wrenne's point of view, it took Matrina forever to finally teach her vocal toning. She may not have understood why there was so much foundational work; after all, she was a singer, but it was because Matrina wanted her to have the deepest possible understanding of what toning actually was, how it was different from singing, how it worked, and the effects it could create. While anyone can learn to tone (in fact, it is as natural as breathing), not everyone understands its nuances, benefits, and potential power. Now that you have stepped through the first seven gates of sound, you have the foundation necessary to truly appreciate the art of vocal toning. (And if you've skipped ahead to this chapter, naughty grasshopper, so be it!)

Toning is a form of singing that anyone can do. Seriously. Anyone. In toning, there's no such thing as being out of tune, and with the exception of a few rules, there's no such thing as doing it wrong either. That said, there are many methods and styles of toning that can make this very simple and accessible art form quite complicated. I will do my best to start with the simple and work towards the more complicated, but please remember, toning is easy-peasy!

Let's start by talking about some of the many benefits that toning provides the body, mind and spirit. Like singing, toning helps increase our oxygen intake. We simply have to breathe more deeply. This in turn enriches the blood and vitalizes our organs. Toning also helps to release endorphins, elevating mood and uplifting the spirit. Toning provides a workout for the face, abdomen, diaphragm, and intercostal muscles. It can reduce pain and stress as well as improve sleep. It improves one's ability to listen and the quality of one's voice. It can combat fatigue and headaches. And perhaps best of all, it is a risk-free, economic, easily accessible means towards enhanced physiological and psychological well-being… without a prescription!

So what are those few rules you'll want to follow when toning?

1. Don't force things. Toning should be light and easy. There's often a temptation in groups to push one's self or to compare yourself to others, but this is counterproductive. In fact, I've seen toning taught as some kind of yelling competition. This is a gross misapplication! That's not to say you can't employ the variable of volume, though.

2. Remember that toning is perhaps more about listening than it is about sounding. Truly. Whether you are expressing on your own or in a group, the ability to actually hear yourself and others is a key component in taking toning beyond entertainment and into the realm of spiritual communion. If you recall, Wrenne had to raise awareness of her ability to listen (Gate 6) before Matrina would even teach her how to tone.

3. Make room for silence. Every second of every toning session, especially in groups, does not need to be filled with sound. There's no need to rush. In fact, sometimes, it's nice to just sit back and breathe if alone or to enjoy

what you are hearing when in a group. At the end of every session, honor the potent silence that follows for as long as you are able.

POSTURE

Toning can be done in any position. During Toning for Peace Circles, participants including myself are known to sit in chairs or on the floor, stand, lie down, or even dance or do yoga. But there are some things to consider that are supportive to the voice. Obviously, having the spine erect when sitting or standing can assist with breath control and help free up the mechanisms associated with sounding (diaphragm, vocal chords, etc.). If you slouch, you'll find it more difficult to control your sound and miss out on the conditioning toning provides. If you point your chin up or down (reaching for those high or low notes), you may be adding unnecessary pressure to the larynx. So just relax and let the head sit naturally on the shoulders. Relaxation while being pulled up through the spine is the key. Even if your tones are short at first, quite naturally, your tones will become longer and clearer without effort.

Experiment with Toning in different postures until you find the most comfortable position for you. I highly recommend intuitive movement when you are toning. Allowing the sounds to inform the body and the body to inform the sounds is a wonderful way to assist in the release of held energies and to deepen your practice.

WARM-UPS

The following basic warm-ups can be practiced every morning or right before sounding. They help prepare the body for the work to come. Toning and working with sound can take a lot of courage, especially in groups. These warm-ups help us relax and be more receptive to whatever may come out of our mouths.

PRACTICE ONE

TOP DOWN WARM-UPS

It might be helpful to think "top down" in order to remember the sequence. Start with the jaw. Using your fingertips, feel for the little indentations between the upper and lower jaw about an inch in front of your ears. You'll know it when you feel it because one fingertip will fit nicely. Slacken your jaw and give a little massage. The area may be very tender; it will love the attention. Now move the jaw very gently up and down and side to side. Don't overdo it. We're just getting a sense of the range of motion there. If you have a very tight jaw, you may also want to try this. Sitting in front of a table or desk, put a pencil between your teeth with the incisors just over the top of it. Now place your elbows on the table, and while you hold the pen, drop your lower jaw open, your hand keeping the pencil in place behind your front teeth. Breathe and relax. Breathe and relax. Put your weight, the weight of your head, on the pencil allowing the jaw to just let go.

Now let's visit the tongue. We are better able to articulate when it is relaxed and flexible. So, here we go. Oh, and this one can get messy! First, stick your tongue out as if you were trying to touch your chin with it. Now flex the tongue up as if trying to touch the tip of your nose. Do the same stretch from side to side. Good. Here's the messy part. Pretend your face is covered in whipped cream. Begin by swiping your tongue over your upper lip stretching it to get as much of the whipped cream as possible. Continue clockwise towards the side of the mouth, the bottom lip, the other side and back up. Now reverse directions. If you aren't getting wet, you aren't doing it right. Make contact with the skin. I told you it was messy!

This next one is a favorite with clients probably because I always do it with them, and they get to laugh at me! First, open your mouth and pop your eyes really wide. You should look beyond surprised. Hold that stretch a moment. Now, do the opposite. Scrunch everything up. Scrunch your mouth, close your eyes tight, furrow your brow. Pinch. Pinch. And release. Relax.

Now let's do some neck rolls. Obviously, there are many muscles in the neck which can, if tight, pull on the vocal mechanisms. So, it's important to stretch. If you have any physical issues which prevent you from doing the following exercises, adapt them to work for you. Imagine there is a string pulling your head up and off of your shoulders. Maintain that sensation of extension and begin by dropping your head towards your chest letting it go as far as is comfortable for you. Now gently, very gently, roll your head around to your shoulder and to the back, open your mouth slightly as you roll back, now to the opposite shoulder. And back to the chest. Good. Let's repeat that in the opposite direction.

One more for the neck. Gently drop your head left, ear to shoulder. You can pull down with the right shoulder to accentuate the stretch. Hold for about 30 seconds breathing deeply and relaxing. Bring your head back to center. Okay, now right, ear to shoulder. Hold. In addition to pulling down on the opposite shoulder, you can also place your opposite arm behind your back palm facing out. Okay. Back to center. Relax in the result.

Our next warm-up is to give the shoulders some shrugs up and down. Bring your shoulders towards your ears. Squeeze and hold. Squeeze and hold. Release. Now just push your shoulders downward and away from the head. Feel the back muscles tighten. Hold. Hold. And release.

Our final warm-up is called Chi Gong Shakes. For this one, you will need to stand up feet about hip-width apart. Now spread your toes into the floor and really feel grounded into it. Begin to bounce your body with little pulses as if you were standing on a trampoline. Continue this movement for several minutes. When you stop, stay completely still, eyes closed, and get a sense of the chi moving throughout the body.

PRACTICE TWO

HUMMING

Humming is a great way to warm up the vocal chords and prepare them for sounding. It's easy too. We all know how to hum. You can either hum a simple tune you know, such as *Twinkle, Twinkle, Little Star*, or you can hum something that has a secondary benefit such as Do, Re, Mi, which also activates and cleanses the chakras. You can improvise a melody based on what you feel in the moment. Don't force it. Be easy about it with a low to moderate volume. See if you can direct the sound into the nasal mask, the area behind the nose and cheekbones. Humming gives the body a sound massage because the vibration is inwardly directed. As with every practice, there are many variations available here limited only by your imagination. For example, you can place your hands over a part of your body to direct and/or feel the vibration there as you tone. You can also try plugging your ears to accentuate the sound resonating inside you.

PRACTICE THREE

MOANING & GROANING

Now that the chords are warmed up, let's take a few minutes to talk about groaning and moaning. First of all, bring to mind times when you would naturally hear someone moaning or groaning, and I'm referring to sounds made here, not the content of speech! When do people groan? Usually when they are in severe pain or discomfort. But they could also be experiencing pleasure. Groaning is a release of pent-up energies. How about moaning? Typically, we moan when pain or pleasure is more consistently present or drawn out. When we are in a weakened, vulnerable state, we moan... whether we're weakened by grief or by the world's most incredible piece of chocolate! There is a definite energetic difference between moaning and groaning. One of your tasks now is to discover some of them for yourself.

Using groaning and moaning with intent, we can assist our bodies to purge blockages of stale energy or emotions. You know, when we are young, we don't think twice about making these kinds of sounds. When we grow older, we become socially conditioned to restrain ourselves from letting go with indelicate or attention-getting sounds. A completely natural and healthy process becomes inhibited by the mind. As a result, all that energy and emotion that would normally be discharged on the sound gets stuck and jammed up in our systems. We're carrying years and years of this stuff around with us!

I remember years ago hitting my head very hard when my landlord happened to be in my apartment. I wanted to scream bloody murder and cry like a big baby. But I didn't. I was too embarrassed. I held it all in. The pain was excruciating for two days, and I was pretty sure I would end up needing a doctor if I didn't do something. I finally started allowing my body to make the sounds I had held in. I felt immediately better, but of course it still took me days to completely work out what could have been released instantly! Live and learn.

As you work with groaning in the week ahead, try experimenting with the zzz, grrr, rrr, and vvvr sounds. As you moan, use the sounds of mmm and nnn. If you find yourself bearing down as you make the sounds, which you will initially, see if you can relax and really let any tension go. There is a clear shift that you can feel between resisting the groan or moan and melting into it. See if you can create sounds that feeeeel reallly good and seem to rise up with a life of their own instead of ones that you contrive.

This is a good time to return to your journal. How have the warm-ups felt so far? Which do you prefer? What have you noticed about your body, your voice, your thoughts, your breath as you walk through this gate?

Toning Basics

Toning is as unique as the individual expressing it. So there isn't one right way for everyone. It isn't about being right or wrong. So be curious. Have fun! If something doesn't feel good, alter it. It's about experimenting and honoring what's true for you. If you find yourself wondering, "Am I doing this right?" – change the question. Tell yourself, "That was interesting." Then ask, "Can I do this yet another way?"

~The Unknown Mother

Toning can encompass so many different types of practices that it would behoove us to spend some time discussing this. So far, you have engaged in humming, groaning and moaning. These can be considered preliminary toning practices rather than toning itself. The heart of toning is working with the vowels, combinations of vowels, and short syllables... like the all-famous OM.

Straight Tones A, E, I, O, U

The smallest elemental units of language are vowels (a, e, i, o, u) and consonants. Without vowels, consonants would be very difficult if not impossible to produce. Vowels are the vessels of consonants and the wombs of potent healing energies. The simplest forms of toning focus on the vowels. We'll get into the respective vowel sounds more deeply in a moment.

Once we add consonant sounds, we are toning syllables which add a completely different feeling to our experience. The consonants M and N, for instance, add a calming, nasal quality to our sounding. The consonants H and K tend to add explosive/solar plexus power. R and Y add a grounding element. There are also chants or mantras, and then actual melodies containing strings of lyrics. Each form of sounding has its place, power, and purpose.

In all languages, there is a meaning for every letter and

combination of letters which we call words. Words are channels of energy which we infuse with meaning. There are different levels of meaning beginning with denotation or the external meaning of words. This is followed by connotation or the personal and associative meaning of words. But there is also a secret (or hidden) meaning to words. It is said that when one understands the secret meanings of words, one has unlocked the mysteries of the universe. Remember, Cymatics has shown that ancient Sanskrit syllables produce the same geometric shape again and again, and in the case of "OM", a shape that these same peoples used to graphically represent the sound. This helps us keep in mind three things. One, ancient syllables arose in a culture that had a greater awareness of sound. And two, sounds are what shape matter. And three, we are unfortunately somewhat removed in present day language from the mystical powers of language.

According to the late Ted Andrews, author of *Sacred Sounds*, vowels were often left out of many early alphabets. It was believed that the vowels contained a power that was dangerous if released carelessly. He also describes the Chaldean alphabet, a predecessor to our own, as a tool for attaining wisdom. So while letters are just little figures on a white page, what they represent is extremely powerful. Letters began as sounds and were transformed into written units. The sounds are what carry the power.

PRACTICE FOUR

Let's look more deeply at the vowel sounds, long and short. The long vowels say their names, AEIOU. As you work with them, you will find they are not as straightforward as it seemed at first. A makes A and E sounds. I makes I and E sounds. O makes UH and O sounds. And U makes Y, U and OO sounds. The short vowels are easiest to understand in the context of a word, so we'll focus on the main ones, AH as in amen, EH as in enter, I-UH as in intelligent, AW as in octave, and UH as in understand. Some people have a very difficult time distinguishing or even isolating certain vowel sounds. If this is true for you, try having someone tone each vowel directly into your ears.

Give yourself some time to experiment with the sounds of the vowels. You needn't try anything fancy. Start with the long vowel sounds, one at a time on a full exhalation. How does each feel? Where do you feel it? How does one, say A, compare to the other, say U? Do you resonate with one more strongly? Is one more uncomfortable to work with? Then move on to each of the short vowel sounds. Ask yourself the same series of questions and record your responses.

Play with the transitional sounds within one vowel sound. What do you notice? What happens, for example, when you stretch the UH that initiates the O long vowel? Or when you stay on the OO of the U long vowel? Experiment with curiosity and observe with detail.

PRACTICE FIVE

FREE FORM VS. STRAIGHT TONING

We've just talked about vowels as straight tones which are single vowels. Many toning traditions make use of straight tones because it really is powerful to stick with one simple sound when harmonizing the physical, mental, and emotional bodies. But when it comes to expression, nothing can bring more freedom than free-form toning. Free-form toning allows for greater variations of sounding. Let's compare straight toning to free-form toning:

STRAIGHT TONING

- can be done alone or in a group
- hones our listening skills
- resonates the bodies (physical, mental, emotional, etc.)
- provides all the benefits of singing

- more restrictive
- tends to focus on pure vowels and more specific syllables
- typically one pitch per exhalation
- is more disciplined
- straight forward

FREE-FORM TONING

- can be done alone or in a group
- hones our listening skills
- resonates the bodies (physical, mental, emotional, etc.)
- provides all the benefits of singing
- allows for more variety
- includes an endless combo of syllables/sounds
- can change dramatically within one breath
- can include rhythm-making (tapping, clapping, etc.)
- lends itself more to letting go
- is more like singing/utilizes more improvisational skills

Free-form toning can have a deep impact on one's physical, mental, emotional and spiritual bodies allowing the practitioner to shift into altered states of consciousness. Free-form toning requires that we let go. The more we do it, the deeper we are able to surrender. In that state of surrender, we open ourselves to both give and receive messages from the Divine, unadulterated by our egos and mental constructs. We begin to trust and obey a deeper impulse, one that arises not from habit, right or wrong, punishment or reward, but rather from essence. We make discoveries. We become enchanted.

Done in a group, everyone is free to discover his or her own path within the framework of toning. It is wonderful when you can bathe yourself not only in your own voice, but in the collective voices of others as well, each expressing individuality. Because it is beyond language, I find myself able to relate to each person present in a much deeper way. It is a universal language.

Free-form toning gives everyone involved an opportunity to experience Oneness and Individuality at the same time.

What arises spontaneously is always different because the group is always different, and it is always perfect. And the group becomes the teacher. What happens is a metaphor for our daily lives. We clash, we crash, we arise from the flames, we soar, we merge, we clash again, we compromise, we rediscover ourselves, we reclaim our power. We enter joy, peace, love, and light itself. This is the promise of free-form toning with others.

Challenge yourself to explore the world of free-form toning. You can start, if you like, with straight tones and then obey any arising impulse to modify your tones by adding a consonant or changing the pitch midstream. Create a melodic chain of tones. Clap, tap, or employ a rattle to accompany you. Open and surrender to the life that longs to express itself in your very own voice. If you can, find some friends willing to explore this with you. Together, take a sounding adventure in which anything goes.

In your explorations with toning, consider the following questions in your journal:

Does the tone feel "right on" or does something feel off? Can you identify what that is? How can you modify the exercise so it feels right? Do you feel the sound not just in your physical body, but in your energetic body as well? Where and how? What qualities does the energy have? Is it balancing, exciting, energizing, calming, heating, cooling, or even draining? Do you feel more aligned and in harmony with life? Does that feeling last and, if yes, for how long after you practice? Does any sensation change as you tone? Do you notice your body wanting to move or dance with a sound? Do you feel inhibited in any way? Are you resisting an exercise?

VOCAL TONING MEDITATION (VTM)

So, on to the basics of Vocal Toning Meditation. The point of VTM is to take the terrestrial act of vocal toning into the multidimensional world of intent, thereby increasing your personal frequency (Gate 7). In so doing, we can remain for longer and longer periods in that higher energy, even when dealing with our everyday lives. It gives us access to all that resonates at these higher frequencies and helps us ground these energies and information into the earth grid. It may sound far out there. And it is far out there. It is beyond what we know and requires opening up to experiences that lie beyond the mind. We are altering our state of consciousness through sound in order to make these altered states the norm... not for the sake of "feeling altered" and not because there is something "better" about such a state. Rather, we are simply opening ourselves to ourselves, filling our vessels with light.

Let me address fear for a moment because, believe it or not, there are many people who experience it when they begin to tone. It is natural for fearful feelings to arise when we are experiencing something new and unfamiliar. It is also natural for suppressed fears to rise as we awaken to more and more of our own light. We're not sure what is happening and our mind has no way to categorize, slice and dice, and otherwise explain what is going on. It, the mind, doesn't really like that feeling. But it is completely okay. There are no dangers in VTM. I repeat, nothing bad can come of your practices. You will always only ever encounter yourself. And while that can be very challenging, it is always worthwhile. And the support is built into the practice. The more you take refuge in the sounds, the easier your shifts will be. Though it may be too much for some, I encourage you to close your eyes when you are toning. It will deepen the inner journey.

Movement is an important element to VTM. But here, I am not speaking of a particular set of movements or a prescribed sequence. The movement arises spontaneously in you as you sound. Allow it. You may find yourself doing some really beautiful and delicate gestures, stretching, and dancing, or you may just suddenly feel like standing up, or sitting down, or weaving and bobbing. This motion will ultimately assist you in navigating the space and time shifts that sound creates. They will also help you ground energies into your body and/or help you focus your intent.

Focus is important. But you are not going to be focusing on some "thing". Sure, you'll set your intent, and you'll be perhaps thinking thoughts about the practice or noticing what is happening in your body, but your focus will be remaining aware. This takes practice. It takes practice to let go of mental control, to allow thoughts and ideas to drift through the mind like clouds, especially those niggling little judgmental ones. But the more you let go, the more and more you will find yourself embodying presence. That's the focus.

And just as you will allow movement and thought, it is also important to allow the sound. You have your own palette. Part of this work is learning to sense where you are and where you want to go... not you the mind, but you the being. Even if there is a facilitator or group with whom you practice singing an EE on a low note, that doesn't mean you can't go for it if you are just dying to soar higher! One person may tone a bright, sustained OH while you feel utterly compelled to whisper an OO, so honor that impulse. As long as you are listening and responding authentically, you are on the right track. If it doesn't feel right once you've done it, you can modify. You can only know by risking, by trying, by modifying.

Sure, you do need to spend time learning the pieces of the practice as they are taught. There is a foundation-laying period where you will be integrating the numerous elements into a coordinated whole. And as that happens, you might feel quite uncoordinated and unsure of yourself. But eventually, you'll get to let go and fly free. For some of you, you may find your wings fairly quickly. For others, it may take a more concerted effort. Trust the process. Trust yourself. This is not a competition. Every moment is THE moment you've been waiting for.

I think we're ready to begin. First, I'm going to teach you a breathing technique which is central to my Transformational Voicework which we'll discuss in more depth later. I call this breath "topping off". Breathe out all your air through your nose. Now breathe in through your nose. When you have taken a full breath, take in just a little bit more air forcefully through the nose in a sniff. Now hold that for as long as you can but not so long that you start to wonder when you can exhale! Exhale when the pressure begins to feel uncomfortable. This is a key element in VTM.

Let's sit with our backs straight. From this sitting position, feel free to move your arms or legs or head, but remain sitting.

Next, we choose a sound to tone. For our exercise, we will tone AH. AH is the sound of the heart. Place your hands over the heart; that is where we'll be directing the energy. Placing the hands on the area of the body to which you are directing the toning helps to direct your intent. Our intent is just to send some yummy energy to the heart.

Now inhale, silently sounding the tone in your mind. At the top of the inhalation, take in just a little more air, now hold, hold, just long enough to feel pressure build, not long enough to feel nervous, and exhale while toning the sound aloud. Don't worry about how the tone sounds. Allow it to express itself; it will evolve as your energy shifts. Sometimes this happens immediately, and sometimes it can take more time than you have available in any one sitting. Just do your best. Use your imagination to visualize the sound traveling the many dimensions of your heart center.

As you empty of air and commence the next inhalation, take your time. You may even take more than one breath before sounding the next tone. When you do, keep things easy and light. Force nothing.

Continue this meditation for about 11 minutes. At the end, use the silence to just be and direct the energies that have arisen to your heart using any supportive visualization, such as a blossoming lotus.

SO JUST TO REVIEW THE STEPS:

1. Assume a toning position whether sitting, standing, or lying down.
2. Choose a sound to work with. This can be any sound, vowel or syllable, a mantra, or even a phrase of intent.
3. Begin by placing the hands on the area of the body where you would like to focus the energy and set your intent.
4. Inhale, top if off, then hold. Release the sound right before the point where holding becomes uncomfortable.
5. While you are sounding, visualize the sound traveling. Take your time at the end of the tone to inhale once or twice before repeating.
6. Continue for at least 11 minutes.
7. At the end, remain in silence and empty yourself of yourself. Pay attention.
8. Direct the energies that have arisen towards your intent using any visualization to assist you.

PRACTICE SIX

Following the steps outlined, create a Vocal Toning Meditation for yourself.

Record your process and results.

PRACTICE SEVEN

SEED SYLLABLES

The following explorations use what are called Tibetan Seed Syllables. They are very potent sounds that contain powerful energies. When you invoke the syllables, you are calling upon these energies to work within and without you.

You may want to plug your ears with your fingers or even wear earplugs to feel the vibrational energies as they are working within your body.

First inhale. Enjoy the beautiful sound of air entering you. At the top of the breath, just when you feel full, take in just a little more breath. Hold the breath just long enough to feel some pressure building but not enough to feel nervous, and then exhale. Now chant the following Sanskrit seed syllables, one for each chakra, all on one exhalation in sequence.

1 LAM
2 VAM
3 RAM
4 YAM
5 HAM
6 SHAM
7 OM

Experiment on your own with the seed syllables, singing one at a time, then mixing and combining them into strings of melody. You may repeat one or more in your "sentence" as in OM YAM YAM OM. Notice how each one resonates within you and where it resonates. Notice how certain combinations feel good to say, like a balm on our hurts or a boost of energy when we feel tired. These sounds are very powerful! Enjoy your discoveries and be sure to record in your journal any personally potent combinations you discover.

How does it feel to work with these seed syllables in comparison to simple vowels? Is there a seed syllable with which you resonate more so than the others? Why do you think that is?

PRACTICE EIGHT

Chi Gong Tones are softly or internally sounded, but also very powerful. Each tone has a body position or posture that goes with it. I have seen many variations even of these tones and positions, so I will repeat Matrina's favorite caveat: there is no one right way to tone. Learn the basics and then modify them according to your inner knowing, interactions, and desired results.

First to introduce the sounds...

Kidney "ch-way"
Liver "ssshu"
Heart "hhhhaa"
Spleen "hhhu"
Lung "ssss" or "sshhh"
Triple Heater "shee"

Now, let's take each one in isolation and practice it along with the body position. First the kidneys and "ch-way". Sit in a chair bending forward as far as comfortable. Now, with each hand, bring your fingertips together as if you were an Italian saying,

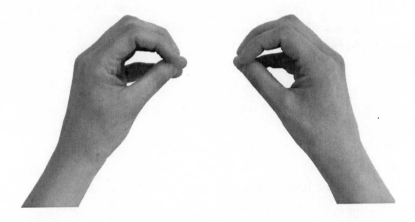

"What's a matta for you, eh?" This is called the Mukula Mudra or "beak hand". Bring your hands to your back about waist level and place your joined fingertips over your kidneys. Make the sound "ch-way". You can experiment to find at which volume to repeat it. You also might prefer to tone it rather than say it, and you might change its duration as in "chhhh... way". As you do this, imagine that any stagnant fear and negative energies are leaving you through every pore. You feel lighter, more at peace.

Now the liver and "ssshu"...

Still sitting, you will keep your hands in the Mukula Mudra. Place your left hand at your sternum and, with your right hand, brush downward from right below where the left hand rests down along the right edge of your ribs as if you were trying to light a match. You'll be moving your fingers from the center out at an angle. Now, as you do this motion, sound "ssshu". Again, play with the sound until it feels good to you. Imagine your liver is being cleansed of anger, hatred, impatience, and other aggressive vibrations. Feelings of centeredness and strength replace them.

Let's go on to the heart and "hhhaaa"...

Sitting, raise your arms overhead, hands clasped, palms towards the ceiling. Stretch and breathe in, exhaling with the sound "hhhaaa". Imagine that nervous tension and agitation are being exhaled. That's it. Allow your heart to relax. Allow a sense of calm to radiate from your heart and fill your entire body.

Ready for the spleen? "Huu..."

This one is just like the liver, only the right fingertips are gathered at the sternum, and the stroking with the left hand is down towards the left side of the rib cage. As you make this motion, make the sound "huu". Use the sound to let go of anxiety. All your worries are released and you feel calm and light.

Time for the lungs "ssshhh"... (or if you prefer, "ssss")

Again, fingertips together. Place the right and left hands on the respective right and left sides of the body about two inches under the collarbone and two inches off center. Make the sound "ssshhh". Allow the heaviness of grief and sadness to be released. Enjoy the sensation of breathing and surrender to the expansion and contraction as your spirit lifts. Be happy. Side note: mothers are natural shh-makers when their children cry. We have somehow twisted this sound into meaning "hush", but really the "sshh" soothes and relieves grief.

And finally, the Triple Heater with "shee"...

Western Medicine doesn't speak of the triple heater. So just to introduce the concept, it is a meridian or energy channel that regulates body temperature and cell function. A healthy immune system relies on a well-functioning triple heater. For this exercise, you may sit as before or lie down. Grab your left ring finger with the four fingers of the right hand. The right thumb will be pointing downward, so if your thumb is on top, switch the right hand so the pinky is on top and the thumb towards the palm of the left hand. As you hold your hands in this position,

sound "sssheee". Repeat three or four times and then switch your hands so that your left hand now grasps your right finger. Repeat. All the while sound "ssshee" to vibrate your entire being, releasing tension and negativity, filling your body with a happy, buzzing light energy.

How did you experience each of these sounds? What physical sensations were present? What emotions? How does the practice change if you whisper the tones? If you internalize them? Which do you prefer and why?

PRACTICE NINE

TONING YOUR NAME

Would a rose by any other name really smell as sweet? There is a great deal of power within a name. First of all, the name itself as it sounds carries a certain frequency. Then there is the power within the sound of each present vowel. And then there is the traditional meaning of the name, and finally, there is the personal meaning and associations.

Chanting your name to yourself can help you uncover the secret energy treasures within your name. There is a well-known practice within toning circles of chanting names. This can be done in all manner of ways, with each person chanting her name into the group and the others echoing this back, or everyone chanting just the vowel sounds within their names all at once, or even one person in the center of a circle receiving his name as it is chanted by everyone else. There is a soothing and healing gift within this practice.

What if you have always disliked your name or just feel energetically detached from it? Well, if you dislike your name, chanting may help you cultivate an appreciation for it. And often, hearing others chant it can restore it to its original power template free of any negative associations you may have.

What if you just do not resonate with your name?

I believe that names should help us remember who we are and where we are going. Names should reflect our service to the world. But often our given names just do not fulfill this purpose.

When I had just turned 38, I was in a near-fatal car incident. I was driving home late at night when two coyotes crossed in front of me on the freeway. I slammed my brakes and spun out of control as my life really did flash before my eyes. It was a strange time-space suspension experience. When I finally stopped spinning, I was facing oncoming traffic on the freeway. By miraculous protection, I was able to right myself and pull over. The odd thing was, I had no fear. As I was pulled over on the shoulder, I heard myself say, "Just take your time. Relax." But I already was relaxed. My heart wasn't even racing. When I woke up the next morning, I had a knowing that I had to change my name.

About this same time, I was reading *The Fifth Mountain* by Paulo Coelho. In it the prophet Elijah experiences a death of sorts of his old life and so chooses a new name to reflect his new life. His purpose becomes his name. Whatever name I received, I wanted it to reflect my purpose.

So, I spent the next couple of months nameless. I shook off the trappings and energy of my old name and awaited the revealing of my new name. I had been reading *Being and Vibration* by Joseph Rael in which he writes that the name of humanity is Drinking the Light. I liked that phrase. It spoke to me of my truth. But I was not about to go around calling myself Drinking the Light. So I waited some more.

About this same time, my job contract ended, my lease was up, and I was freshly divorced. So I packed up what I could fit in my car and drove away following a call into my new life. Somewhere on the road between Ohio and Pennsylvania, I heard a voice say, "Giselle." My reaction was, "You have got to be kidding me." But the voice was insistent, so I just sat with it for a while. Giselle turned out to be a hint. The rhyming Dielle was the answer, a derivative of Drinking the Light. Only later did I learn that Dielle held additional meaning that pointed to the service I am here to provide.

Not everybody wants or needs to change their name of course. But I encourage you to consider the symbol of your name and whether or not and in what ways it serves your life... or maybe even limits you. And if you find your current name somehow lacking in energy for you at his time in your life, ask to receive a new one, one that will remind you of your truth. It will be given. It is up to you whether or not you use that name secretly or publicly or at all.

Now, spend some time toning the vowels in your name or even your full name. Note any observations or feelings that arise. If you can find a willing volunteer, tone the name of a friend or loved one. Ask them what they felt. How did you feel making this offering on their behalf?

PRACTICE TEN

TONING FOR THE PHYSICAL BODY I

In order to work consciously with the body, first we have to learn to listen to it. A good technique for learning this is to engage in conversation with a problematic body part. For example, let's say you are experiencing shoulder pain. Begin by saying hello to your shoulder and that you would like to have a chat. Ask it what it is trying to tell you and then let it take over. Become the voice for your shoulder. It might sound something like this.

"Hello, my sore shoulder. I feel how upset you are. Please talk to me and tell me what is going on."

"I'm so angry, I don't feel like talking!"

"Why are you angry?"

"I'm angry because you overused me yesterday. You asked too much of me and now I'm hot and sore."

"I'm so sorry. You are very loyal to me. Thank you for your service. How can I make it up to you?"

"I want ICE!!!"

You get the idea. Trust yourself. The conversation might make sense and it might not. That's okay. Let it be what it is. You may find yourself hitting upon a great insight into your pain.

If you feel resistant or silly listening to your pain that way, you can converse through toning. One way to do that is to employ the siren technique for identifying and alleviating pain in the body. To do this, begin sounding your deepest tone possible. As you raise your voice up the scale, take note of the pain and any shifts that happen. Maybe you hit a certain note and you feel a twinge or spasm. Maybe you feel a cool sensation or heat. Maybe the pain even dispels. That is a sign from your body to hang out at that pitch some more, while being attentive to any changes. At some point, the sound might just naturally rise or fall in pitch, or even change. Allow it to guide you. Don't try to steer it with your mind.

The human voice is capable of so many different sounds. Experiment with your vocal palette and the various consonants and vowels to discover the state of your physical being. If you aren't sure where to begin, begin with a sigh and let your voice stretch and express from there. Notice how certain sounds resonate with certain parts of the body. If you have a pain, explore sound as a means to connect with, decrease, and maybe even increase the sensation. The idea here isn't to bring yourself more discomfort, but just to touch upon a knowing that sound does affect matter. Try something totally new. Get experimental.

How in touch do you feel with your body? Is it easy to understand its messages? It is easy to give it access to your voice in order for it to express itself? Why or why not?

PRACTICE ELEVEN

TONING FOR THE PHYSICAL BODY II

Toning with movement is a great way to help get yourself into your body. You can tone with movement as a way to shift pain or discomfort or simply to become more aware of yourself. Let's practice a toning that involves physical movement. We're going to explore the tones OH and OO in this exercise. Stand up and be sure to give yourself plenty of elbow room. Begin by doing a few chi gong shakes really feeling the feet grounded to the floor, the toes spread out and relaxed. Now begin to gently tone the sound OH and allow your body to break from the pulse of the bounce into any movement it wants. There is no right or wrong movement. Small is okay. Big is okay. Hang out with OH for awhile and notice how your body responds with movement. Now, change to the sound OO. Notice what happens. Does your movement become faster, slower, bigger, smaller, more stretched, more detailed? Hang out in OO for awhile. Now gently bring your body back to the chi gong shakes. That's it. Gently pulse the body and return to your center. Now relax and enjoy the energies moving through your body as a result of the exercise.

Create or modify your own toning with movement activity and record what you did and how it felt.

PRACTICE TWELVE

TONING FOR THE EMOTIONAL BODY I

The following practice can be done when one is feeling a particular emotion or network of emotions as a result of some trigger or situation. In a way, like we did with the body part conversations, we are giving a particular emotion a voice. In doing so, we may discover some insight into our belief system or even a resolution to our problem. So begin by inviting your emotion into a conversation. It might sound something like this:

"Hello, great big ball of anger! You sure are powerful! Can you tell me why you are here?"

"You know why I'm here. That jerk cut me off."

"Hmm… is that really what made you arise? Is that such a big deal?"

"Well, humph, it's just that I was in a hurry. Now I'm late!"

"Is that scary?"

"If I'm late for this meeting, it will make a bad impression."

"Why would that be bad?"

"Because I hate feeling incompetent in front of my boss… it's not my fault!"

As you continue, you may discover a great deal of insight into your emotion. You may discover that your emotion is enjoying being the center of your attention. You'll find it just wanting to vent, so let it out in all its intensity, but then it will shift as it feels heard and accepted. And you may realize that you have a belief buried deep down that isn't really serving you anymore. I like this activity because you remain the witness (and parent) to your emotion. It doesn't overwhelm you and take over your identity. If you find that happening, the story may just be too intense for you right now. So return to it another time when you can put some space between yourself and the feeling.

If you are able to converse in a meaningful way with your emotion, the next step is to love it through action; in our case, sounding. Begin by imagining that the very center point where you feel the emotion arising is being filled with light. Breathe into that space sending it healing, acceptance, forgiveness, and deep peace. Imagine it glowing and breaking apart, dissolving into the light. Now sing yourself a series of nurturing tones. Try the vowels preceded or followed by SH, M, N, or F.

Fear is really at the base of every negative emotion. When I say "negative" emotion, I assume it is clear that no emotion is "bad". They all merely guide us to truth. I'm using the term negative to refer to the less comfortable states of being... and some of these can actually be very desirable. We're just not comfortable feeling them! At any rate, fear is a mighty powerful force. We can use toning to help shift or alleviate our fear.

Imagine a situation or thing in your life that brings up your fear. Maybe you are afraid of speaking in public, for instance, but have to give a speech for work. In your body, allow the feeling of fear to arise in its intensity. Notice any heat, pulsing, or shifting energies in the body as you do so. Explore with your voice the state of your emotional being. Whatever your emotional state when you begin, simply take note of it, and without any effort to change it, get experimental with various sounds. If you aren't sure how to begin, just pick a vowel... let's say OH. Tone an OH and pay attention to how it feels... what emotions may arise. From there, begin to play with different sounds. What do you notice? Do certain sounds lift you while others seem to pull you down?

Do you find yourself having an easier time with your physical body than you do your emotional body or vice versa? As you play with more and more practices, are you finding yourself a little freer with your voice? Is it easier to experiment? Record any noticings in your journal.

PRACTICE THIRTEEN

TONING FOR THE EMOTIONAL BODY II

When we are feeling an emotion, it is a true indicator of our thoughts and authentic self. Toning is a great way to get in touch with our feelings, and for many people, it is far less threatening than therapy. You can use a tone to convey an emotion. You can also listen for an emotion and become better skilled at discerning the related harmonics.

When exploring toning of the emotional body, it is helpful to create a long list of emotions and related "feeling" words, or words that are related to feelings to refer to. You can use the Internet to get a master list, but then spend some time personalizing it with your most experienced emotions in one column, your least experienced in another, and those that fall in neither column somewhere else. Then, use the following syllables: AH, AY, HOO, HEY and experiment toning each syllable with a different emotion. Let's say you have "frustrated" on your list of emotions. Tone the sound AH as if you felt frustrated. You are doing two things. You are releasing, and you are being more fluid in both holding and moving through emotional states. Try to make the sound as authentic as you can. In other words, don't force it. It might be helpful to call up an image or event to bring the emotion to the surface. As you tone, notice where you feel it. Notice how you feel it. And if it shifts midstream or you find yourself wanting to change the sound, follow that impulse. Then move on to AY, HOO, and HEY. Begin by exploring the emotions with which you feel most acquainted and see how that feels. Then move into those that are more difficult or less common for you to experience. What's the difference in where and how you feel them? Do you notice any resistance? Then consider whether you think the emotion in question is pleasant or unpleasant. Do you feel blocked in expressing a particular emotion?

The series of sounds, AH, AY, HOO, and HEY represent both yin and yang. AH and HOO are yin, the feminine, receptive sounds. AY and HEY are yang, the more masculine, direct sounds. Do you notice that certain emotions are more easily felt with the yin or yang syllables? How do these yin yang aspects affect your process with each emotion?

After you have spent some time working with your list in this way, you can then begin to use the words Yes and No. Again, explore and notice what arises. If you say yes with the emotion of frustration, where do you feel it? Have you felt that in your life before? Can you say it another way and shift the feeling?

PRACTICE FOURTEEN

TONING FOR THE EMOTIONAL BODY III

Laughing is a wonderful emotional release and studies have shown that laughing, even when initially forced, lifts mood and leaves one feeling better. It may be related to the body taking in more oxygen, but I believe it is also a result of the physical displacement of stagnant energies within the bodies: physical, emotional, and mental. Generally, we laugh with HE, HO, and HA. Do a three-minute laughing exercise. Just do it. Push through any resistance or feelings of silliness.

How did that feel? How do you feel now vs. how you felt when you started the exercise?

PRACTICE FIFTEEN

TONING FOR THE EMOTIONAL BODY IV

Another way to work with the emotional body is with music. Select various pieces of music and create an emotional playlist for yourself. Then lie down and listen allowing the music to call up whatever emotion it evokes. If you feel playful, you can even do this activity standing and "hamming" it up, dramatically overplaying each emotion. Just feel into the music and how it entrains you. If there are lyrics, what role are they playing in the emotion? If it is instrumental, what about it is evoking a certain emotion for you? Can you practice feeling the opposite emotion while listening? Between each selection, pause and notice if there is any residual emotional pull. Just notice and acknowledge the power music has.

Write about your experience.

PRACTICE SIXTEEN

TONING THE MENTAL BODY

Now, let's explore the mental body. Start with something simple. For example, focus on toning the sound of EE. Feel it resonating in the head. Continue for several minutes and then pause. Notice how you feel. Then experiment with other sounds.

Which sounds can quiet and still your mind? Which can bring you more alert?

PRACTICE SEVENTEEN

VOCAL CARE

There are lots of ways to care for the voice. This week, spend time every day doing just that. Suck on horehound candy, purchase a soothing throat spray, practice silence, do stretches for the neck and shoulders or even get some bodywork for that area. Practice

the Shankh Mudra, hum lightly when you shower inhaling all that steam, and abstain from irritants like smoking or drinking. Drink lots of water!

In what ways have you failed to care for your voice in the past? What do you plan to do now to rectify any abuse? How does it feel when you honor and tenderly care for this aspect of yourself?

The 9th Gate

Attunement

The Gate of the True Voice with a capital V flies open and calls us in. It asks of us to dive in deep into the sea within. Diving deep, we free ourselves of unnecessary strife. We recover here a voice inspired by unadulterated, pure Life. No longer seeking outside ourselves to know we are okay, we find the courage to finally express and triumphantly have our say. Earth, air, fire, and water, and of course ether too, combine and blend to purify, so we may express with voices new. Tears, laughter, snorts and hoots, they all are free to come, until at last we rest in the quiet of knowing we are all one.

TRUE VOICE

I am a servant of Sacred Sound. I place myself in complete trust when and where I am meant to give this gift. No matter what passes my lips, as long as I'm aware, it becomes a prayer. Each syllable – each tone – is imparted with intent to heal, inspire, and evolve those in its presence. With awareness, even hello or no thank you become passages to enlightenment. With my voice, I open channels – new channels, not those deeply rutted and entrenched channels that you've been taught are the only channels. No, my voice embodies all possibility. It's beyond observation and can only be experienced in each moment. My voice is as unique as a fingerprint. I don't try to sound like anybody else or impress people. In my voice is a life – Life itself. My voice – and yours too – is a living being, a pulsing form directly linked to the Divine. When I allow that divinity to flow, I am no longer Matrina. I am immersed, One with the Creator. I sing it all into being.

~The Unknown Mother

TRANSFORMATIONAL VOICEWORK

When I first developed Shamanic Voicework, as I called it then, I was hesitant to introduce it in my groups. I knew it was very powerful stuff, and there were only a handful of clients who I felt were ready for it. When the time was right, I started introducing this work in groups, and I have to say, the results astonished even me. What you will learn in this chapter is a process only mentioned briefly in *The Unknown Mother*, presented for the first time in this book. You will learn the breathing techniques and three main processes of Transformational Voicework (TV) accompanied with stories, video links, and tips to assist you in your practice.

Everything up to now has been a preparation; and here at the 9th Gate, we begin to put it all together in a series of processes that bring us back to our True Voice. Having said that, it is important that you feel ready to undergo these processes. I recommend that anyone who has difficulty coping with their emotions or energetic self hold off or else work through this chapter with a qualified guide or therapist.

In yoga, the throat or Vishuddha chakra is considered the purification center of the body. It governs expression and our mental forces, both our inner and outer voices (our thoughts, even if unexpressed, impact our bodies with their energies); it's how we speak and how we listen; our personality and how it shines out into the world. It is considered the transformation center, the power to open the physical mind to the light of the divine consciousness. In TV, we work intentionally with the purification center and a series of processes that utilize breath, movement, and sound to help activate and clear the entire body. TV works directly with the vocal channel (Gate 1) helping to reestablish its natural ability to expand and contract depending on the situation, bringing it to a state of absolute authenticity.

This work has proven itself again and again, with one-on-one clients and in workshops, to move massive amounts of blocked and stagnant energies. Unprocessed emotions are given safe passage up and out of the body, and often a joyspring and laughter are found underneath.

The Breathing Techniques

There are three very specific breathing techniques which I employ in TV, each one eliciting a different response from our nervous systems (generally speaking as there are always exceptions, and of course some of you may find one more to your liking than another). Topping Off you've already learned, but we will revisit it and each of the others.

TOPPING OFF

This was introduced at the 8th Gate. Remember? In this breath, you begin by exhaling completely. At the very bottom of the exhalation, inhale fully. At the top of the breath, pause just a moment. Then take in a little extra air. Now hold this breath to just before the moment of discomfort.

This breath is where we start and great to return to when you feel stuck or resistant to the process.

I've been asked about why I employ topping off as part of the work. What does it do? For one thing, it puts us at our edge of comfort. We are holding the breath, suspended. It is like holding a beach ball under the water in a swimming pool. Eventually, it will release and bring with it a rush of energy. We use this rush to bypass our inhibitions with sounding. In a way, by holding the breath we are also confronting our fears.

http://youtu.be/vpEUAcz_cOE

SOBBING BREATH

The Sobbing Breath is one that helps us process emotion. We begin by taking several short, quick, forceful inhalations through the nose until full, then exhale with brief bursts in a sigh or cry on a vowel (refer to Gate 8) out the mouth. It will sound just like someone sobbing. Each time you do it, you can try a different release sound until you hit upon one that resonates with what you are feeling. The important thing here is to inhale deeply like a baby about to wail. And on the release, keep your face as relaxed as possible.

This breath is great to do when you begin to feel emotional as it helps facilitate the emotional release without the clinging or resistance that often accompanies emotion.

http://youtu.be/AhLnKAumP6U

CYCLIC BREATH

The next breath helps put our resistant monkey-mind to rest

whenever it rears its head during our sessions. To do it, inhale but exhale before fully inhaling. Then inhale before fully exhaling, and so on. Repeat this process at the most comfortable pace you can maintain. The idea is NOT to hyperventilate, so if you feel as if you are, back off. Take longer breaths in and out. You may feel dizzy, so utilize this breath when you are lying down, or in other postures, only once it's become second nature to you. The exhalation will generally be longer than the inhalation, especially as you start to vocalize on each exhalation.

This breath is perhaps the trickiest of the three, but it is by far and away the most powerful once you feel your way through it. And only you can do that! When you do, you'll discover a momentum of releasing sound on each exhalation... just be sure to allow the sound its full life. Don't censor yourself or cut it off abruptly before its time. In other words, if the exhalation is no longer in rhythm with the inhalation, that's perfectly okay, and in fact heading in the right direction. Let the exhalation... the expression... take over. Once you become more adept, the intuitive mind will take over helping you with the balance between pushing yourself to express on each exhalation and stopping to breathe normally in order to integrate everything that is happening.

This breath is great to do whenever you feel directionless within the process. If you find yourself thinking too much or wondering what it is you are supposed to be doing... or whether you are doing it "right"... employ this breath.

http://youtu.be/0MPUW80KyZ4

Try each of these breaths and notice how they make you feel. Record any thoughts, confusions, questions, and observations. Once you are comfortable with these, you are ready to enter the first of the TV processes.

MOVEMENT

We are almost ready to go into each of the three main processes that combine sounding, breath, and movement. However, let me say a word about movement before we do. The movement of TV, while it can be stretching-, yoga-, or chi gong-type moves, is left to the individual, or to be more accurate, the individual's body. It is not prescribed movement, but intuitive movement different for everyone and arising from the natural impulse of the body. We simply honor our body's desire to move... like a cat stretching in the sun or a dog shaking off the wet from the river.

The key to this intuitive movement is to remain aware of doing it. Should you find yourself holding the same position or making the same movements over and over, take it as a sign you are stuck and immediately try something different. We want to break patterns, not reinforce them. These movements don't have to be large. They can be micro-movements... the wiggling of a finger, a nodding of the head... all used to get in touch with ourselves and what might be lurking in memory within the tissues and bones.

Spend some time for the next few days just allowing the body to move intuitively for five to ten minutes. You can do this to music or in silence, but try not to let the mind direct the movements. Let the body move the way it wants. Music can be helpful if you find this difficult because you can surrender to the rhythm to inspire the movement. It's a step closer to letting the body "speak for itself", a process you began at the 8th Gate. Keep practicing. Eventually, you'll be able to move without self-judgment or distracting thoughts.

How does it feel to allow your body to move intuitively? Is it easy? Difficult? Easier with or without music?

MY TRANSFORMATIONAL VOICEWORK PROCESSES

PROCESS ONE

CHAKRA BALANCING

The first process in TV is a chakra clearing and balancing one. It's a great place to start, being less intensive than the following two processes. If you aren't well acquainted with the chakra system of the body, I suggest your investigations start there. In fact, this will be essential as we move into the 10th Gate. Many excellent books have been written on the subject such as *The Sevenfold Journey: Reclaiming Mind, Body, and Spirit Through the Chakras* or *Wheels of Life: A User's Guide to the Chakra System* by Anodea Judith.

The chakra process is done seated. You can sit crossed-legged on the floor or in a chair with your feet flat on the floor, whichever is most comfortable.

Begin by focusing on your breath as you breathe in and out several times normally. When ready, do a practice Topping Off breath. Then place your attention on the root chakra at the base of the spine. On your next inhalation, imagine your breath taking the shape of a ball within your vocal channel, moving downward towards the root; once it lands (see note below), let the energy disperse and permeate throughout the root where it begins to work like a sponge or magnet seeking out and then soaking up anything and everything you no longer need to retain. Let it build as you hold the breath. See the ball reforming in your mind's eye, saturated with stale and unexpressed energies. When you are ready, you will release this ball on your exhalation, without even having to think about it. It will rise with the exhalation and be expelled out the mouth with a sound.

You will repeat this practice at least three times at each center, progressing up the basic seven chakra system... root, reproductive area, solar plexus, heart, throat, third eye, and crown.

Note: You may find that when you visualize the sphere of the breath traveling down the vocal channel that it only gets so far. If this is the case, you have a blockage that should be dealt with rather than attempting to take things all the way into the root (or whatever chakra). Likewise, there may be times in your practice where you want to work through each of the chakras, but you only get up to the solar plexus, and that's as far as you seem to get. It is important to pay attention to and honor these momentary limitations. The body knows what it needs and its capabilities. Trust your intuition and obey the body rather than some idea of "I have to get through all the chakras" or "There is a particular order to which I must adhere."

Pay attention to the types and qualities of sounds that you release on each breath. Before moving onto the next chakra, take a moment to compare for yourself any differences between the three sounds expressed. Was one more "authentic" than the others? Was one longer or fuller? Were they all similar and difficult to distinguish? Did anything surprise you?

Each time you sound, see if you can allow the most fulfilling expression you can possibly muster to arise. I often refer to a satisfaction scale of one to ten with my clients, one being a sound that feels forced, faked, truncated, or blah, and a ten being one that is completely satisfying, full, surprising, and yummy. Obviously, you want to shoot for the tens! Initially, the common thing is for people to express sighs rather than sounds. It's all part of the process. But do recognize there is a difference between sighing and toning. We're ultimately after the fully- vitalized breath of tones.

Doing this activity in a group is one of the best ways to fully comprehend authentic sounding and vocal palette because others demonstrate and mirror so much for us. It is often easier to pick up on things observed in others than it is to see them in ourselves. So if you can, find some friends willing to explore with you or get thee to a workshop!

How was this activity for you? What did you notice as you progressed through the chakras? Did your breath travel all the way down to the root or stop somewhere along the way? Did you feel a change in the body as you held the breath? What did you feel when you released? How satisfying were the sounds that you released?

PROCESS TWO

EMOTIONAL BALANCING

When we are little, we have a great fluidity with our emotional states. In one moment, we may be crying with anger or frustration, and in the next we may be giggling with delight. We drop our emotional states and transition into new ones with ease because we are operating free of much of the baggage we later pick up about expressing our emotions.

This next process is meant to help us move through our emotional states with utter fluidity. It teaches us a great deal about how we hold ourselves rigidly and also how to return once again to a neutral state... with ease.

First, give yourself plenty of space as you need the freedom to move and sound. Once established, begin by imagining yourself surrounded by a sphere of protection that has a membrane through which we can control both what comes into this sphere and what goes out. This membrane offers 360 degrees of safety on all sides and dimensions.

Now, choose an emotional state such as anger. Allow your body to take on anger and notice how your posture changes. Notice where in your body you tend to hold this emotion. Notice also any subtle changes in body temperature or breathing rate. Begin to use your voice now to give expression through sounds (words are okay too, but try not to get too inside the mind or story). Use the breath and the movement to evoke the sound from up out of the body. Really feel it and fully express it. Then, in an instant, drop the anger and bring your body back to a neutral state. Release the posture. Become still. Relax. Feel neutral.

After a moment, take on another emotional state such as joy. Feel joy in the body and notice how your posture may change. Express joy on the voice. What do you notice? Is anything difficult? How does this all compare to the energy of anger? Really let yourself go fully and completely into joy. Then, in an instant, drop joy and bring your body back to a neutral state.

You can continue in this way for several minutes, going from one emotional state to another. A list of emotional states is included below to help give you some ideas, but you can find many additional ideas on the Internet. You may want to select the emotional states in which you often find yourself getting stuck or the emotional states of others that tend to pull you in and off center (remember entrainment?). By doing so, you are strengthening your ability to move more fluidly in the actual life situations in which you find yourself on a daily basis.

You can also take this activity deeper by being more and more dramatic with your movements and sounds. Really go for it! Spirit will be there to support you through it. When I work one-on-one with clients on this process, we are able to go quite deeply into energetics stored within the dimensions surrounding the body. It isn't something easy to describe in writing, but suffice it to say, it is always surprising to discover just how much of ourselves we hold outside of our awareness... segments of our soul cut off for various reasons such as trauma or unsupportive mental constructs.

Suggested Emotions: anger, fear, shame, pity, envy, joy, sadness, wonder, courage, impatience, trust, confusion, embarrassment, resentment, grief, denial, compassion, nervousness, vulnerability, disgust, gratitude, frustration, impatience, awe.

How was this activity compared with the previous process? What did you notice about each particular emotion you worked through? How did your body respond to the emotions? Were you able to find neutral easily? What kinds of sounds did you find yourself making? Were you able to express what you felt through the voice?

PROCESS THREE

CATHARTIC RELEASE

The most powerful of all the processes is one most like the practice of recapitulation briefly mentioned in Gate 2. In fact, this is the process which developed out of my work apprenticing on the Toltec path. It helps move tremendous amounts of energy in the body, even the most stagnant of old, congealed energies. Let's face it. If our energy is stuck in the past, we don't have the resources we need in the present. With this process, that energy becomes available to us once again, making change and growth easier. By adding sound and movement, it goes further than traditional recapitulation to really help the nervous system reset and reprogram itself.

What can you expect from a session? As I mentioned earlier, there were times after completing a session of this work where I nearly floated off the floor for feeling so light, or felt so connected to the earth it was like I was thirty pounds heavier, both quite pleasant sensations letting me know that I had moved some serious energy. My clients and workshop participants have described similar experiences including more challenging ones such as light-headedness, coughing, crying, and yes, even vomiting. Don't worry, that is the rarer of the effects! The important thing is that by doing the work, one moves into a state of purity. Clients and participants also experience fits of laughter or joy, buzzing sensations in the body, an increase in heat, and spontaneous song. All or none of these might be your experience.

This is the process which coordinates the three breath techniques, movement, and free-style toning. It's a lot to put together, so go easy. You will probably feel uncomfortable at first, and without a facilitator at your side, unsure whether or not you are "doing it right". Trust in the process itself to inform and guide you. Call upon Matrina to support you. Take it slow and pay attention to all the subtle responses in the body. Then modify your practice as you go.

You will need to be in a place where you will not be disturbed and where you can feel free to make whatever sounds may arise. Give yourself at least 10 minutes but as long as you like for this. Twenty minutes is an optimal amount of time, but the longer you can stay focused, the deeper your experience.

Find a comfortable place on the floor to lie down. You may want to cover yourself with a blanket to keep chills off. It's best to be flat, but if you need to prop yourself with pillows for comfort, do so. This is about honoring your body, not conforming to some prescribed way of doing things. Pay attention to the direction of your head with the crown pointing where you feel most supported.

First, set your intent. Why are you doing this? Do you want to release some particular block? Do you want to open up to some new form of expression? Do you want to get in touch with some aspect of yourself that feels isolated or rejected?

You will begin by allowing three normal breaths. When ready, commence Topping Off. With each release, you will be sounding and allowing the body to move as it wants. Then, on to the next breath. Pacing is important here. Don't waste any time. Go right into the next breath – unless you feel exhausted or in need of integrating. Then you can pause. If you begin to feel emotional or perhaps like emotion wants to come but is stuck, switch your breathing pattern to the Sobbing Breath. Continue for as long as you feel fed by it. If you are in your head, trying to figure things out, or the opposite, totally unfocused and confused, move to the Cyclic Breath. Just keep breathing and keep moving for the entire period you've set aside to do this, only taking integrating pauses as necessary.

You may feel a great deal of heat building. That's normal. You may feel a little dizzy. It's all okay. The floor is there to support you. Rest if you need to at any time. You may want to ask someone you trust who is good at holding space to sit at your side while you do this. For some of you, that may create a greater inhibition, so just do what works for you, balancing your need for support with your need for privacy.

After the appointed session time, simply be still and breathe normally.

GROUND WITH LIGHT

It is important after each and every session that you bring your body back to a neutral state. (You practiced this in the Emotional Balancing Process; if it has been difficult for you, please return to that practice before you proceed.) With your intention, simply decide to drop whatever might have arisen and return to neutral. Then breathe and feel into all the new, empty space created in your body. We are going to fill this space with light. Using your inner eye, imagine a white-hot sun above you with its rays pouring down. Allow these rays to penetrate your aura and body, filling all that space with glorious, healing light. Allow it to permeate every cell and fiber of your being programming all that space with new information for a freer, happier, more light-filled you. Rest in that light, breathing and grounding yourself before you get up. Take your time. There's no rush. Be sure to get up slowly. Contents may have shifted during catharsis! ;)

HOLDING BACK VS. EXPRESSING VS. RELEASING

There are different categories of sounds that tend to be made during TV. These are holding back, expressing, releasing, and transcending, each with its own quality and signature that a trained practitioner or perhaps someone with more experience would be able to point out to you. If you are working alone, I offer this description so you can place part of your witnessing attention here.

Sounds of holding back are often truncated. Those listening get a sense in their own bodies of something shutting down or being suppressed. It is apparent that the mind has entered the process making the sounder hesitate or cut off the sound before its full expression. The body, especially the face, reveals a great deal about whether someone is holding back. Rigidity in the limbs, stagnant postures or gestures, tightened face muscles, and the gritting of teeth are sure signs that one is closing down on what wants to be expressed. Should this happen to you, a great technique is to simply open the mouth while relaxing the face. Move the body by shaking the arms or rocking your legs. Sounding should come easily... not take tremendous effort. Only holding back takes tremendous effort.

A word about screaming: For years, I facilitated these groups out of my home which provided a more intimate atmosphere than, say, a dance studio. When I would demonstrate some of the sounds that might arise during the work, I would always joke that the police hadn't shown up yet. Often, someone would ask me about screaming. My response is that it depends upon the scream. There are some screams that signify holding back and these types of screams are not good for anyone. They can injure the voice and completely break containment within a group. The way the body is held during screaming is a very good indication of whether a scream is of benefit or not. The body should be loose or, if experiencing tension, moving that tension through intuitive movement. Screams that arise and that are releasing are not bloodcurdling, eardrum-shattering shrieks. They are more grounded into the body and do not bring physical discomfort to the vocal chords.

Sounds of expressing can be gritty, indigenous-sounding, and heavily emotional. Those listening can feel a sympathy in their own bodies, even an empathy for those prone. Or they may instead feel an irritation as the sound resonates within them with something they have yet to bring into awareness. For those sounding, expressing can be a trap. One can be lured into losing one's self to the emotion. It is important to remember the practice of one) maintaining the witness and two) of shifting back into neutral regularly.

Releasing sounds tend to be extremely satisfying both to the maker and the listener and are the sounds for which we are striving when we are stuck in holding back or releasing. Think back to the satisfaction scale. Sounds on the lower end of the scale might feel incomplete, short, unfulfilling. Sounds on the higher end of the scale feel more full, rich, and satisfying. Often, they have a longer duration and more power behind them. Always aim to make sounds that you would rank higher on the satisfaction scale.

Transcending sounds are just that. They are like a balm on the wounds from which other expressions spring. They can be quite angelic or reminiscent of a mother singing to her child. It can also be expressed as laughter. When a client starts to laugh, often uncontrollably, the sound of that laughter can tell me they have reached pay dirt. Soft tears are also a sure sign that the alchemy of Transformational Voicework is taking place.

SOME TIPS

1. Many people get stuck in releasing sighs rather than sounds. That is fine at first. Eventually, though, you want to move past this phase and actually engage the vocal cords. If you find it difficult to allow actual sound, try keeping the mouth open before exhaling. Anticipate that sound will come out.

2. Another great trick is holding the fist at the solar plexus and applying pressure on your exhalation. Use as much pressure as you can muster in this area of the will that retains our fear and inhibits our expression. Pressing down here as you sound helps to free any stagnant energies there which, in turn, helps facilitate the

allowing of sound.

3. While you should allow the breath to spread throughout the body, you should also make sure that you aren't releasing it unawares. "Allison" was a client who would practice her topping off breath, and oddly, when it came time to release the breath, there was nothing to release. She was basically seeping breath the whole time she was holding it. When we talked about this, she came to realize that it was a lifelong habit. She was always seeping her energy and always tired. Working with the breath turned her onto a pattern she had established at a very young age, one that wasn't serving her. We then focused on her maintaining the inhalation.

4. Have a box of tissues handy! It is more likely than not that you will be releasing emotion, if not from some repressed grief or fear, then from the awe and divine connection that can result from this practice if you've already done a lot of inner work. In fact, that *is* the ultimate purpose of this practice: to realign us with our divine nature and begin to express from that.

5. If you can find some friends interested in exploring these processes together, I highly recommend group work. There is so much benefit and balancing gained. One person who is more inhibited hears another who is free with volume, and suddenly new possibilities open up. One who has trouble feeling emotion hears another begin to cry, and suddenly either the floodgates open, or they feel purified by their neighbor's tears. We all help each other process and move through things as one body in groups. It is fascinating.

6. Did you remember to bring yourself back to neutral? Be sure to do the Ground with Light at the end of each and every session. Please seek support if something arises

that you feel you can't handle alone. While as spiritual warriors we know it can only be good that things are coming up to be witnessed and released, that doesn't mean you have to go it alone.

How was your initial practice? If you've done it more than once, is it getting easier or harder as you progress? Do you notice yourself holding back with movement, breath or sound? How satisfying are the sounds you are allowing? Has anything surprised you? Did you have thoughts about "doing it right"? Were you able to notice the three types of sounds: expressing, releasing, transcending? What physical sensations did you experience? Did you ground? How do you feel now?

True Voice through Mantra

Mantras are sacred syllables repeated over and over by practitioners in order to both alter their energetic fields to the frequency of the mantra (for prosperity, equanimity, or compassion for example) and to quiet the mind. One well-known mantra is OM MANI PADME HUM, meaning "Hail to the jewel in the lotus." There is a reason this practice has persisted throughout the ages and why it is one adopted by so many of today's self-help educators. Mantras work.

But for some, the foreign language or even religious roots of certain mantras can be hindrances to adopting a practice. Here, I offer a modern mantra practice which can be used in your modern life… one that does not require a knowledge of ancient languages. This practice, when done correctly, will have the same effect as an ancient mantra but it will also begin to build your awareness of the vibrational signatures of the words in our own language.

Ideally, you will want to use this practice when you feel balanced and peaceful. First thing in the morning is a great time to set the stage for the day ahead. But you may also use this technique when you feel the mind turning to worry, or have had a challenging day. Call forth the symbols that you wish to activate. Spend ten minutes saying words like "triumph, peace, love, happiness, release, letting go, stillness, courage, joy, compassion, steadiness, tranquility, friendship, miracles…" Try to choose words directly counter to your present state if you feel perturbed. For example, if you are feeling impatient, try words like "patience, plenty, relaxation, stillness, calm, ease." It's okay to repeat words. Follow each word with a nice inhalation of clean, fresh air. As you do so, allow the mind to freely associate with your life experiences of the words. Allow the feeling states to arise. Notice how your energy field begins to change. You will feel happier, more at peace and much better than you did before.

What we are doing with this practice is using the energy of symbols consciously to generate and radiate their energy in our field. We are aligning with these qualities in order to surround ourselves within a bubble of the light of their protection and direction. Once we invoke these qualities, we have easier access to them. They begin to inform our choices and actions. Now that's the power of the word!

MANTRA PRACTICE I

Adopting the practice of a traditional mantra can teach you a lot about vibration, the energy of words (even if you don't know what they mean), and the power that comes with discipline. You may want to invest in some mala beads that can help you keep track of the number of times you recite your mantra in any sitting, but they aren't a necessity. You can choose a well-known mantra such as Om Mani Padme Hum or Gate Gate Paragate Parasamgate Bodhi Sahva or do an Internet search for a specific mantra that will help you with a challenge you are facing. They can come from any tradition. It doesn't really matter as long as it resonates for you.

Once you've selected your mantra, commit to spending time daily to recite it. 108 times once a day is a good start. Or you might consider reciting at both morning and night times, during the day at regular intervals, or even for an hour or more a day.

When I was deeply engaged with my mantric practices, I was reciting three hours a day every day. It was intense, but the benefit to my mental state was astounding. As I was instructed, I was keeping count of the total number of times I recited the various mantras I was working with, although beyond a certain point, one hundred thousand, two hundred thousand, I no longer cared how many times I had repeated something. Counting started to feel like a distracting burden meant to prove something. I had nothing to prove to anyone but myself, so I let the counting go. My point is that this practice shouldn't feel like a race against time or a numbers game. Keep a relaxed and steady pace and enjoy the process.

Record your experiences with this process in your journal.

MANTRA PRACTICE II

If traditional mantras don't float your boat or you are ready for something different, you can create your own personal mantra similar to an affirmation. Over the years, I've had many different personal mantras including *may the world be free of my judgments* and *may I see, hear, and be the Truth and the Light*. Once you have determined the mantra, you can use it in any or all of the following ways:

- Recite it just like a traditional mantra.
- Write it down and circle each vowel. Then chant only the vowels morphing from one vowel to the next on one exhalation.
- Create a sigil with it.
- Create a mandala or some other artwork to embody the mantra.
- Use your mantra to engage in some voice play. Say it normally, whispered, yelled, deep voice, high voice,

quickly, slowly, slow and deep, slow and high, quick and deep, quick and high...

Listen deeply for the nuances that each change presents in the meaning, feeling, and conveying of the phrase.

Compare your experience with this practice to the more traditional practice. Which did you prefer and why?

MANTRA PRACTICE III

Remember our work with sigils at the 3rd Gate? These verbal spells, something repeated over and over in order to generate a vibratory field suffused with the energy of the intent of the mantra, can be integrated with practices at other gates such as this one. We've so far worked with sigils as written glyphs. But sigils can also take the form of a Mantra. Our simplified example statement from page 41 was:

I RECEIVE CLEAR GUIDANCE

Next, the letters are rearranged in some random fashion. Joseph Max suggests using *Scrabble* letter tiles for this purpose which make it easy to manipulate and rearrange them. The idea is to obtain a series of "nonsense words" using the letters. So one possible combination of I RECEIVE CLEAR GUIDANCE would be:

I RECV LA GUDN

Rearrange the letters into nonsense words such as:

LAGU IDNEC RVVAC DURL NIGE

Choose your favorite combination as your sigilized mantra:

Now you can turn any sigils you created at the 3rd Gate into a mantra or start from scratch with a new one. Then chant the mantra in any way you choose. You can use the mantra with your original glyph or by itself. Again, some people will use the mantra once and then never use it again. I like to play with mine from time to time even creating melodies and recording harmonies with them. But remember, I have by that time blocked the original meaning of the sigil from my conscious mind.

THE 10TH GATE

ATTUNEMENT

Through the 10th Gate we go into the realm of colors and energy wheels. With three eyes open, we dance and spin and weave together a coat of many colors, full of light and electrical power. Stand in the waters of purification and enjoy a rainbow shower. Unifying root to crown, we blend and merge these energies. Radiating every color, we glow and grow in synergy. As far as your imagination can reach is as far as your voice can carry you. Each can help the other stretch and reveal a whole new view. Dissolving old systems and structures, we respectfully progress apace. In the journey to no destination, we are free of running a race. Honor your truth above all else to discover the Rainbow Light Body Grace.

Rainbow Light

We have spent much of our time through the first nine gates emptying and purifying our vessel with breath and vibration. The Rainbow Light Gate is about filling that space, our entire beings, with Light and allowing our true message to be shared (a process begun at the 9th Gate). As we walk through this gate, we uncover the treasure we buried deep within ourselves when we first experienced "the clamp". Burying it was a way to protect ourselves and our very precious gift, preserving it until this sacred moment. Now we have the strength, maturity, wisdom, unbending intent, and, most importantly of all, the inner space to open this treasure chest and shed our Light upon the world.

Practice One

Sun Breathing

On a sunny day, place yourself either indoors or out in the rays of the sun. You can sit or lie down, spreading your arms wide in a receiving gesture. Do not use sunglasses if you can manage. Make sure that you will not be exposed unprotected for any length of time; do not fall asleep! Make sure the light is directly on your face and, specifically, your closed eyes as you begin to focus on your breath. Imagine the rays of the sun becoming aware of you and reaching towards you with love. Feel yourself filling with this light, its energy buzzing over every part of you. You might even want to squint your eyes so you can play with these dancing rays as they approach. Now breathe even deeper, feeling these rays as they penetrate your being, carrying information to every cell, every fiber of your being. Allow the sun to alter and reorganize your system towards wholeness and wellness. Allow its beams to not only restore your heavenly blueprint, but to gift you with information beyond your human comprehension. Know it will be processed by the body in time, and one day express itself into the world as a blessing for all. Do this for at least five and up to ten minutes every day.

How does it feel to Sun-Breathe?

PRACTICE TWO

UNIFYING THE CHAKRAS

Those of you who have done at least six months to a year of chakra balancing work are ready to move into the Rainbow Light Body practices of unifying the chakra system. If you haven't, I refer you back to the work of Anodea Judith mentioned in the previous chapter. Spend significant time working through each of the chakras *before* attempting to unify them. It isn't that you could damage yourself or anything like that; it's just that your efforts will likely have been wasted.

Tone the following sequence, each of the seven vowels closed with the sound of M (UH OO, OH, AW, EYE, AY, EE, M) while maintaining your attention on each chakra, one at a time, beginning with the root. Blend the sounds as you move from one vowel to the other, so that they become one great tone. Work your way up the chakra system to the crown and then come back down to the root.

What kind of chakra work have you done in the past? How has it been helpful to you? What have you learned about the chakras since then? What did you feel after doing this exercise?

PRACTICE THREE

If you have access to a gem shop, find some agate slices in the colors of the chakras. Typically, brown or deep red resonate with the root, orange with the sacral area, yellow with the solar plexus, green or pink with the heart, light blue with the throat, deep blue with the third eye, and violet or white with the crown. Lying down, place the agate slice on its respective chakra, allowing each slice to protect and cleanse that center. Then slowly pull each slice one at a time onto the heart chakra, stacking them, in essence bringing the energy of each chakra into the heart. You can move from the root up or simply use your intuition to bring whichever slice you want to into the heart first. Once you have all the slices stacked on your heart, radiate all the energy in the heart out, expanding it first within your entire body and then out several feet beyond. If you cannot acquire agate, you may use any small stones representing each of the chakras, but you will probably not be able to stack them, and they will be prone to rolling off you.

Practice Four

Create mandalas of art representing a multitude of colors as each of the chakras blends into a wash of rainbow intensity in one. If you don't consider yourself to be artistic (is that still even possible at this point?) and don't have any paints or other art supplies on hand, an easy way to do this is with old magazines. Select images within each chakra color scheme that speak to you. Then arrange these images in a pleasing fashion and display them for yourself to enjoy.

Practice Five

Over a month-long period, each week, meditate on each chakra, one per day, using your intent to begin to dissolve the boundaries of that chakra. Let their energy expand and overflow. If this feels comfortable, great. If it feels like too much, contract the energy back to a more comfortable place, and just keep stretching. Upon the completion of each week, as you start the next week, begin to run energy up and down first from the root to the second, then the root to second to third, then the root to second to third to fourth and so on. You will be creating a very strong channel that will help you connect and align all chakras, making their energies available to you when needed.

What are you experiencing as you begin to run energy in a different way? Is it having an impact on other practices you are doing? Is it impacting your expression?

Practice Six

Similar to the Sun Breathing, let's now fill ourselves with color. Fill your entire body with light, begin with red, then orange, then yellow, then green, then blue, then purple and then white. Get a sense of the rainbow radiating from the center outward in all directions, behind you, above you, below and in front. Place your hands on your respective chakras in the following order:

Heart (open and connect to love)
Forehead (empty your head of all knowledge)
Womb (feel the fire in the belly burning)
Root (feel juicy, alive, and excited)
Feet (allow life to flow in and used energy to flow out)
Throat (feel open and free)
Crown (allow light to pour upward and in)

Experiment with more non-traditional colors. Play with silver and gold, pastels, opalescent tones, and other shades. Use your *ever-growing inner knowing* to guide you to the colors that best serve you at this point in time.

What colors speak to you the most right now? How does each of the colors of the rainbow make you feel? Are there certain colors you prefer to wear than others? What colors surround you at work? In your home? What colors seem to be lacking from your life?

Practice Seven

Experiment with color. Redecorate or paint a room. Purchase something in a color you love even if you don't think you can "wear" it. When you see a color you love, breathe it in. Then see if you can hear it.

PRACTICE EIGHT

IMPROVISATION I

Nothing strikes fear in the minds of men and women more than having to improvise. For many, it is laced with feelings of incompetence, loss of control, and embarrassment. But really, the ability to improvise, the grown-up version of "playing", is the ability to open oneself to divine inspiration. Hopefully, everything you've been doing up to now has been opening up that vocal channel and giving you a newfound courage when it comes to just letting it out! Like many of my clients, you may find yourself less inhibited in your daily life, able to confront matters more assertively, and more prone to creativity and joy.

It's time to take a few new risks and discover a new art form you've always thought belonged to others. For an idea of where to start, think back to the times you've said, "I always wanted to..." or "They make it look so easy; I could never..." Try painting, poetry, pottery, sculpture, piano, guitar, dance, moviemaking... something you've never done before. *The Artist's Way* by Julia Cameron is a great resource to turn to for motivation and encouragement.

Need inspiration? Look no further than those you most admire, the greats, but use that inspiration not to copy what you see or hear, not to belittle your own attempts, but to express yourself and your unique perspective. Notice and respond to what you notice. Respond with colors, sounds, shapes, words, and movements. Sure, the mind will do its thing, trying its hardest to inhibit your expression until it "knows" what to do. Use that self-doubt and even fear as grist for the creative mill. Trudge through it. Just jump in and modify as you go. Fly by the seat of your pants! Remember, there are no mistakes, only learning opportunities.

Improvising in one arena makes it easier to improvise in multiple arenas. Since you've been working with the voice as a tool for creative expression, keep the momentum going:

When you find yourself in a space with fantastic acoustics, play with toning or singing.

Make up songs in the car as you drive about what you are thinking and feeling. You can also make up songs at home, about making the bed or chopping vegetables, or at work, about writing those e-mails or making those calls.

Does the idea of improvising scare you? Would you rather have a plan or instruction? What art forms call to you? As you engage with your chosen expressive art, what do you notice? How do you feel? Is there any resistance? What are the voices in your head saying? How does it feel to let your inner child play?

IMPROVISATION II

When I used to teach creative drama to children, one of my favorite improvisational games was taking ordinary but odd-looking objects (I often didn't know what they were myself), passing them around the circle, and having each person answer

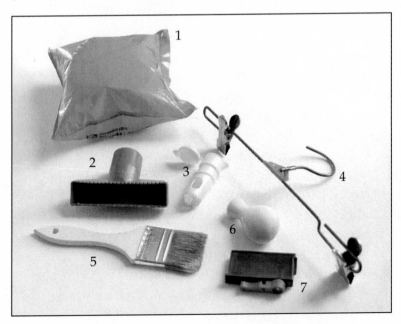

the question, "What else could it be?" Try it. When you come across an interesting "thing", come up with at least three things it could be. Be as creative as you can. The idea isn't to come up with three ideas of what it could really be... but rather, what it could be if anything were possible. Here's some inspiration to get you started in reference to the items pictured on the previous page:

1. a whoopie cushion
2. cinematic-vision attachment for a periscope
3. a cheap jeweler's loupe
4. Spanish Inquisition nipple torture
5. a invalid bowling pin
6. a mascara brush for the Statue of Liberty
7. the backside of a Barbie slot machine (midget One Arm Bandit for our UK readers)

PRACTICE NINE

GLOSSOLALIA

Glossolalia, otherwise known as "speaking in tongues", has its roots in ancient tribal and religious practices. The idea is letting go, sometimes into a trance-like state but not necessarily so, and allowing Spirit to speak through you. I greatly debated whether or not to include glossolalia here; Matrina does mention it and later works with Wrenne on the practice. However, it is so very jaded with connotations of insanity or religious extremism that many people discount its value, seeing it as totally weird and discomforting to witness, let alone try for themselves.

The fact is, there is something powerful and mysterious going on within the act of glossolalia. But the more scientists study it, the less mysterious it becomes. Glossolalia alters brain chemistry in such a way as to imply that it helps us deal with things we cannot grasp intellectually. Recent research at the University of

Pennsylvania School of Medicine has shown just how glossolalia affects the brain.*

Those speaking in tongues experience a marked decrease in frontal lobe function (this is opposite of what meditators' brain scans show) and an increase in activity of the parietal region. The former area of the brain enables reason and self-control so glossolalia involves a surrender or letting go. The latter region takes sensory information and tries to create a sense of self relating to the world. So glossolalia may help us make sense of our experiences in life.

I have always been able to feel something happen in my brain, as if a switch is suddenly turned on... or perhaps off... that helps me leave the world of thinking and knowing and enter a world of simply being and receiving. For myself, and many others, gentle tears often accompany this switch.

I have used glossolalia in some of the recordings I have made over the years to convey messages that could not be put into words. I have also used it as a practice to increase my ability to just let go and surrender to life. I know of others who have taken the art further, actually using it to access guidance for themselves or others, bringing it back into this world, and then translating it into a language we can understand.

However it might be used, glossolalia can and does open a doorway to pure information. When processed through the heart, that information remains clean and crisp, but like anything else, the messages can be tainted by the filters through which they pass. That's why I prefer to keep glossolalia a private practice one does for one's self.

There is a lot of initial discomfort for people when talking this way. It may feel like silly gibberish, and I guess from a certain

---

*Newberg, A.B., Wintering, N.A., Morgan D., Waldman, M. R. *Measurement of Regional Cerebral Blood Flow during Glossolalia: A Preliminary SPECT Study.* Psychiatry Research: Neuroimaging, 2006; 148 (1): 67-71.

perspective, it is. But the point is what that practice of making gibberish is doing for you and whether or not you can allow it to provide you with a rich resource for inner guidance that bypasses your judging, justifying, "need to know" mind. If you can get over yourself and the embarrassment of making strange sounds, you may be able to get in touch with a part of you that is comfortable with and open to mystery. It just may enrich your spiritual life and fulfill a need you didn't even know you had.

As you become more and more comfortable with this practice, use it to quest for information whether you are able to understand or translate that information or not. You can ask for teachings on situations in your life that are troubling you. It's just a tool. Experiment and see what it can mean for you.

Ready to try it?

Create a sacred, uninterrupted space and light a candle. Set your intent to engage in speaking "nonsense". See what happens. Do you fight it? Giggle? Can you let go of the part of the mind that resists? Can you enter a space of surrender? Try closing your eyes. You may whisper very quietly; it doesn't have to be loud.

If you find it difficult to let go, you might want to engage in some drumming, toning or chanting, or even dancing to music that inspires you beforehand. As the thinking mind begins to relax, take the window of opportunity this provides to enter a new world of "tongues".

How did this feel? Did you feel self-conscious? Silly? Were you able to access that "switch" in the brain from left to right? What did you receive?

BEYOND THE GATES

ATTUNEMENT

Let us walk beyond the Gates, into the Unknown together.

Falling we enter in silence, into a dream, where masters transmit Truths beyond knowing.

Look behind the veil, beyond understanding and glimpse what your Spirit is showing.

This is your true home...

this quiet, empty place

this expanse of boundless no-thing.

And now the bells come to life with a joyous, empty ringing!

Can you armlessly embrace a sentence with no words to discover a voiceless singing?

SILENCE

Silence is the stream of intent. Without silence – without ether and space – there would be only an impenetrable void in which our ability to create would cease to exist. What is a drawing but lines punctuating white space? What is a song but notes filling the emptiness? Silence is also the most powerful form of communication.

~The Unknown Mother

On this journey of awakening, we now transcend the gates to cultivate and immerse ourselves in silence. Wrenne originally had a rather strong aversion to the idea of practicing silence. We spend so much of our time running from it. We feel compelled to turn on a TV we aren't even watching, to distract ourselves with constant Internet browsing, or we fill our environments with music. There is nothing wrong with listening to music or anything else, but are we giving equal time to the absolute silence? If not, chances are, we're using avenues of entertainment to avoid something we're sure will swallow us whole. Wrenne overcame her resistance and discovered that the practice of silence was one of the most powerful teachings Matrina had shared.

Are you ready?

PRACTICE ONE

Dedicate time out of each day for silence. Don't meditate. Don't contemplate. Don't think. Don't not think. Just sit and give yourself to Silence. Start with just five minutes if you have to. Shoot for twenty. Do more if you can. Gradually increase the time you spend in daily silence. When you are done, spend some time with your journal. You may just find your pen hovering above the blank page, your mind equally blank. That's fine. Something will come. When it does, write it down or draw a picture.

How are you with silence? Is it difficult? Does it feel uncomfortable? What happens when you sit in that discomfort and don't try to change it?

PRACTICE TWO

In *The Unknown Mother*, Matrina tells Wrenne the story of Echo just before she says goodbye:

A woman and her daughter were climbing the mountain, gathering herbs and medicinal plants. The daughter nearly tripped over a half buried stone as she ran ahead into a hollow. Stubbing her toe, she yelled out in pain, "Oooww!!"

Just then, the daughter heard a cry from the other side of the hollow: "Oooww!!"

Curious, the daughter yelled into the hollow, "Who's there?" to which came the reply, "Who's there?"

This made the daughter indignant, thinking someone was playing a cruel game. This time, she yelled, "You are nothing to me!" And the voice answered in kind, "You are nothing to me!"

The mother, humored by what she'd heard, caught up with her daughter in the hollow.

"Daughter," the woman said. "Pay attention!" Then the mother yelled, "You are beautiful!" to which the voice replied, "You are beautiful!" Then the mother yelled, "I love you!" and the voice echoed back, "I love you!"

The mother explained to her open-mouthed daughter that the voice is known as Echo, but truly it is the Voice of Life: "Life is a mirror of our thoughts, words, and deeds. If you want to have a friend, be one. If you want compassion, give it. If you desire others to be patient and respectful of you, give your patience and respect to them. This is the law."

For at least a week, pay attention to what you give out to the world and notice what comes back. Journal about what you notice and about the insights you glean.

PRACTICE THREE

Use a bell or bowl to enjoy a meditation with silence. It doesn't have to be anything fancy. A metal Himalayan bowl, a crystal bowl, a single chime, Tingshas, even a doorbell will work. Ring the bell or bowl and follow the sound as it drifts into an eternal fade. Allow the silence that both precedes and follows the ring to carry you deeper into stillness.

PRACTICE FOUR

If you can, I highly recommend sitting in silence with others. First, you may want to close your eyes. At some point, practice with your eyes open. Notice the temptation to don a mask whether it be a smile, a serene or tense expression, or one that darts attention from point to point in the room in avoidance. Notice any discomfort in yourself or others. Though it may be awkward at first, with practice we discover a way of relating that is altogether more enjoyable and fulfilling and find that so much of how we related to others (or thought we were relating) has really just been background noise. Really connect by radiating from the golden core of your genuine Light. Melt into the silence and non-doing. Get used to holding this energy of silence in a group so that you can hold it out and about in your world... at work, at home, at play, and in service when called to do so.

How does it feel to sit in silence with others? What masks or anxieties arise for you, if any? What have you noticed in the reactions of others?

A CLOSING WORD FROM MATRINA...

All of life is sound. Only by returning to sound will we be free of form. The voice is a link to a person's power, like a chord or tether from the unmanifest to the manifest. Sound is a bridge between form and formless. If people can learn to walk that bridge between worlds, they will manifest their creations with impeccability. They need to know that sound is love and love is sound. Sound is being. All of life sings and all of life must sing to be healed.

Tell them their hearts are made of music. From the time they're conceived, they are musical. Tell them that colors and words – all are a form of music, a form of sound. Each person, each living thing, is a vessel of sound – each a unique melody. Sound is a palace in which God resides. Sound is a chalice of awakening: The Holy Grail. The voice is an open vessel for the word of God. Each human is that God, creating his reality through his words. Tell them that the word was our way into creation, and it is our return home. Tell them that every note that's played within the body of a human being is a note that rings through eternity, creating the great Nada or All.

Explain that ancient places are filled with sound; their stones retain wisdom through sound, and with sound, we will reclaim the lost wisdom and knowledge. Explain that sound builds and destroys. Sound is God. All of life is the vibration of creation. We must learn to vibrate at increasingly higher velocities if we are to evolve. We cannot continue to take for granted the power of the word if we are to evolve. We cannot take the power of sound for granted, and we can no longer remain ignorant of the power of music to program us.

I really must be going. So take heed. Return to sound. Reclaim the art of sound. Learn to listen with our hearts' ears wide open. Learn to listen once more with the entire body as we did before our birth. Allow our words to arise from nothing rather than knowledge, practice, and habit. Break the backs of the symbols that hold us hostage. Turn our vulnerabilities inside out and let them become our power.

Allow. Surrender. God will speak through you. God will sing through you. And every utterance will heal nations.

~The Unknown Mother

Your journey has just begun, for as you close the pages of this book, you open the sequel, an unwritten book of Sacred Mysteries just waiting for your decisions and actions. With each choice you make in the name of love, forgiveness, respect, and justice, the Truth shall be burned into the pages with a hand of such great beauty and power. I am so proud of you, child, not only for your desire but for your courage to be healed and whole as you prepare to take your place among the gods. Precious creator and healer, what a benevolent ruler you shall be! What a blessing to us all!

Continued Blessings,

Matrina

Afterword

While my spiritual journey has always been a conscious part of my life, my healing adventures didn't really begin until 1995. My ventures into sound healing followed around the year 1999 when I took a shamanic journey to Canyon de Chelly in Arizona. It was a powerful initiation that changed my life. During that journey, my first ever camping trip, complete with five-gallon-bucket "facilities", we were led in group activities using movement, percussive instruments, and voice. There were about 40 of us on that trip, along with a handful of facilitators. One night, I had an experience I'll never forget.

I remember moving my body to the polyrhythms like a jaguar through the crowd. My breathing altered, becoming deeper and more rhythmic, and my vision revealed to me a very fluid world. Everything was liquid, yet I moved through it with ease and grace. At one point, we were told to pause and sing the syllable SA. I didn't know then that SA can be translated to mean both "I am" and "the start of something". It was certainly the start of something for me.

I opened my mouth to begin toning, but through no volition of my own, the sound kept wanting to rise higher and higher in pitch until I reached a crystalline note I never even knew I was capable of making. Tears streamed gently down my cheeks as my crown chakra opened to allow this sound to pour into me and out my mouth. I felt filled with the light of God. I've never been the same since. I believe that Spirit had somehow opened a channel within me allowing me to receive and share this work.

I learned afterward that the sound had not only impacted me personally, but had also served as an inspiration to others present in the group. One woman told me if I didn't keep singing, she would hunt me down and haunt me for the rest of my life. Not one to enjoy being hunted or haunted, I've been singing ever since.

Another important journey in my life took place a year or so later on a trip to Sedona. I went with the intent of receiving information on what I was supposed to do with my life. I had thoroughly confused myself by following too many different paths and interests. I wanted to know why I was here, and I needed guidance. On the very last night, I had a dream I didn't recall. But when I woke up, I knew without a doubt that I was supposed to use my voice to teach others to use theirs, so they too could experience what I had in the Canyon a year before.

As soon as I got home, I started to lead vocal play groups, teaching myself along the way through books and using my intuition to lead the practices. Since I already had a teaching background, I was comfortable leading a group, so thankfully that wasn't a hurdle I had to overcome. Still, I was astounded, not only because people showed up time after time, but because they seemed downright hungry to express themselves in this way.

Since then, I've experienced a handful of other dreams and what I can only describe as activations in which I received sound teachings or empowerments, one of which has been pivotal to my most recent work. I dreamed that I lived in a beautiful, utopian mountain community. Our leader was a master of sound, creating compositions that would propel humanity forward. One day, we heard helicopters circling overhead. Everyone felt apprehensive as the helicopters landed in the square. Men in suits... military, federal agents, secret service... disembarked and began to question people, filling minds with fear. They told us that our world was an impossibility, that we were being led astray by our leader... whom they had come to arrest.

Those who listened began to doubt themselves, to be afraid for their own safety. I got so mad; I knew I had to act immediately. I sat on the steps of the square and began toning, a humble and seemingly innocuous act. It wasn't enough to get the "lie machine" to stop spewing their poison, but it was enough to send a shudder through the crowd, to reawaken them from the "disenchantment". The men in suits eventually realized they wouldn't get anywhere and left in their helicopters.

When I woke up, I knew I'd been given a glimpse of the hidden protective potential within toning. When people practice this form of expression... one that lies beyond words, dogmas, religions, creeds, and divisions... we reclaim one unifying human language... that of love. It's the language we'll absolutely need for us to birth a new human and a new world... one based in sustainability and innovation, responsibility, peace, and unity.

My personal healing journey hasn't just been about sound. I am also deeply steeped in Toltec traditions having apprenticed with several teachers since 2000. These teachings helped me to understand the importance of faith. I worked to reclaim mine, making it possible for me to use sound as a healing, meditative, and spiritual tool. These teachings also taught me about the true nature of love, a power of which I had very little experience and understanding for so much of my life.

A sound retreat in 2003 in New Mexico was another pivotal experience for me. It was my first exposure to Tibetan mantra and sound healing. My studies of Bon Shamanism continued and remain yet another influence in my work. I'll never forget the night I spent after my first gong meditation. My entire being vibrated through my sleep and was still ringing the next day. There was no doubt in my mind that sound was a mystery school I had to enter.

Sometimes, this work is difficult to share, its true depths difficult to communicate. There is so much more to sound than what we hear, to toning than just singing, and to the voice than just speaking. My thrust is to help people peer beneath the obvious in order to discover what sound and its applications might hold for them. Conscious sounding is a form of prayer, a communication with the invisible, and your prayer should always be your own.

RESOURCES

WEBSITES
DielleCiesco.com
ToningforPeace.com

DISCOGRAPHY
Vocal Toning Meditation: Level 1 Foundations
available for download on CDBaby

ABOUT THE AUTHOR

Dielle Ciesco is the author of *The Unknown Mother: A Magical Walk with the Goddess of Sound*, the story of one woman's journey to find her True Voice. She is also the creator of Transformational Voicework and Vocal Toning Meditation and founder of Toning for Peace. She specializes in the transformational power of the voice to heal and connect us with our own Divinity. Passionate about every Voice, be it the one we use every day to communicate, the ones we hear inside our heads, the silent voice of wisdom, voices raised in song, or the ones that call us to awaken, she is a featured improvisational vocalist on the TLC series with Visionary Music, creators of DNA Activation music, as well as on the *Bliss of Being* with Richard Shulman and the Pure Heart Ensemble. With over 18 years experience as a performer, teacher and healing facilitator, Dielle blends her experiences in vocal toning, sacred sound, meditation, Toltec & Bon shamanism, multidimensional music, Reiki Tummo, coaching, and teaching to assist clients in discovering a deeper connection to their inner truth and wisdom. She teaches workshops, writes, sings, makes art, and works one-on-one with clients.

The Unknown Mother: A Magical Walk with the Goddess of Sound

Dielle Ciesco has magically tapped into the sacred shamanic voice that resides deep in the heart of all creation. Matrina, the Unknown Mother, reminds us that sound and words have the power to heal what ails humanity when we are willing to surrender to the Great Mystery.

~Linda Star Wolf, Author of *Shamanic Breathwork: Journeying Beyond the Limits of the Self* and *Visionary Shamanism: Activating the Imaginal Cells of the Human Energy Field*

It isn't every day that one meets a goddess, let alone a Matrika or being that presides over the sounds of language. It is said such deities can bring us complete liberation. Will that prove true for a struggling vocalist named Wrenne when a mysterious woman appears and offers to help her find her True Voice? This beguiling and eccentric teacher guides us all on a deep and powerful journey through 10 mystical gates of sound, sharing great insights, secrets, and profound wisdom about the power of letters, words, and our very own voice to transform the world around us. This isn't standard knowledge; this is a gift for our times, taking the reader into the very heart of sonic revelations.

978-1-78099-631-8 (Paperback)
978-1-78099-632-5 (eBook)

MUSIC

Bliss of Being by the Pure Heart Ensemble
PureHeartEnsemble.com

Transmissions of Light Codes: *Journey Towards Ascension*
Transmissions of Light Codes: *Aya's Underworld*
Transmissions of Light Codes: *5th World Emerging*
available from VisionaryMusic.net

AYNI
BOOKS

"Ayni" is a Quechua word meaning "reciprocity" – sharing, giving and receiving – whatever you give out comes back to you. To be in Ayni is to be in balance, harmony and right relationship with oneself and nature, of which we are all an intrinsic part. Complementary and Alternative approaches to health and well-being essentially follow a holistic model, within which one is given support and encouragement to move towards a state of balance, true health and wholeness, ultimately leading to the awareness of one's unique place in the Universal jigsaw of life – Ayni, in fact.